Special Praise for U

"Claudia Black has written an excellent and accessible book for anyone who wants to understand more about what trauma is and how it may have impacted their lives. *Unspoken Legacy* is user-friendly and easy to follow as it traces the underlying, intersecting ways in which trauma can manifest. Unresolved trauma can be the pain pump that fuels both addiction and relapse. It cuts an insidious, seamless, and all too often invisible path through a person or a family system that over the years and even the generations becomes overgrown, buried, and hard to see. Through case examples that ring only too true, Dr. Black brings to life the myriad things we tell ourselves to either stay in denial or to express the relief that comes when light finally dawns. She elucidates both the path of illness and that of recovery; this is a book that will help many people."

Tian Dayton, PhD
Senior Fellow, The Meadows
Author of *The ACoA Trauma Syndrome* and *Emotional Sobriety*

"One more time Dr. Claudia Black has written a book that is pivotal to helping people understand their history and move forward in their lives. Her gentle voice of experience and compassion offers a multitude of solutions for the problems that affect all those with addiction and trauma. *Unspoken Legacy* is filled with useful exercises to enable the reader to actively engage in the process of healing. Dr. Black has done an incredible job of addressing the complexity of trauma and addiction and its impact on families. Everyone from the professional to the student to those personally affected must read this book."

Mel Pohl, MD, DFASAM
Chief Medical Officer
Las Vegas Recovery Center

"Renowned addictions expert, Dr. Claudia Black has done it again! She's written a groundbreaking guide to help anyone struggling with addiction or the havoc it wreaks in its path. This well-written book offers cutting-edge information about how addiction develops in families, the impact it has on one's psychological and spiritual well-being, the powerful ways in which trauma and addiction are inextricably interconnected and, most importantly, what must happen for healing to occur. Filled with practical insights and do-it-yourself exercises, Dr. Black's guidance is compassionate, informative, and inspirational!"

Michele Weiner-Davis, LCSW
Author of *Healing from Infidelity* and *The Sex-Starved Marriage*

"In this brilliant work, Dr. Claudia Black illuminates the connection between trauma and addiction, the toxic cycle of shame and fear that results, and how this can get passed intergenerationally. Most importantly, she provides a blueprint and road map for help, hope, and healing."

Jerry Moe, MA
National Director of Children's Programs
Betty Ford Center

"Claudia Black's new book is a wonderful must-have resource that's more than helpful for the healing and recovery around trauma and addiction issues. It is a useful educational tool on so many levels, and reminds readers that everyone experiences some level of trauma in their life's journey while reassuring them that healing is truly possible.

Claudia gives many useful mindfulness examples and thoughtful advice for recovery that are truly life saving. The reader will feel safe, reassured, and will find real hope after reading this book.

Unspoken Legacy offers the opportunity to develop skills and tools to live on and live well!"

Karen Phelps Moyer
The Moyer Foundation
Cofounder Camp Mariposa

UNSPOKEN LEGACY

UNSPOKEN LEGACY

Addressing the Impact of Trauma and Addiction within the Family

CLAUDIA BLACK

CRP
CENTRAL RECOVERY PRESS
LAS VEGAS

Central Recovery Press (CRP) is committed to publishing exceptional materials addressing addiction treatment, recovery, and behavioral healthcare topics.

For more information, visit www.centralrecoverypress.com.

Publisher: Central Recovery Press
          3321 N. Buffalo Drive
          Las Vegas, NV 89129

23 22 21 20 19 18   1 2 3 4 5

Library of Congress Cataloging-in-Publication Data

Names: Black, Claudia, author.
Title: Unspoken legacy: addressing the impact of trauma and addiction within the family / Claudia Black.
Description: Las Vegas, NV : Central Recovery Press, [2018]
Identifiers: LCCN 2017020976 (print) | LCCN 2017035366 (ebook) | ISBN 9781942094579 (ebook) |
ISBN 9781942094562 (pbk.: alk. paper)
Subjects: LCSH: Dysfunctional families—Psychological aspects. | Psychic trauma. | Addicts—Family relationships
Classification: LCC RC455.4.F3 (ebook) | LCC RC455.4.F3 B5273 2018 (print) | DDC 362.29—dc23
LC record available at https://lccn.loc.gov/2017020976

Photo of Claudia Black by Winifred Whitfield. Used with permission.

The American Society of Addiction Medicine (ASAM) definition of addiction on page 30 is used with permission of ASAM. Copyright © 2017 American Society of Addiction Medicine. For more information, please go to https://www.asam.org.

Every attempt has been made to contact copyright holders. If copyright holders have not been properly acknowledged please contact us. Central Recovery Press will be happy to rectify the omission in future printings of this book.

Publisher's Note: This book contains general information about trauma and addiction and the interaction of the two on family systems. It represents reference material only and is not intended as medical advice. This book is not a replacement for treatment or an alternative to medical advice from your doctor or other professional healthcare provider. If you are experiencing a medical issue, professional medical help is recommended. Mention of particular products, companies, or authorities in this book does not indicate endorsement by the publisher or author.

CRP's books represent the experiences and opinions of their authors only. Every effort has been made to ensure that events, institutions, and statistics presented in our books as facts are accurate and up-to-date. To protect their privacy, the names of people, places, and institutions in this book have been changed.

Cover design and interior by Deb Tremper, Six Penny Graphics.

In memory of Jack Fahey,

my husband of thirty-nine years,

the love of my life.

TABLE OF CONTENTS

ACKNOWLEDGMENTS

Special thanks to:

The many clients who over the years guided my understanding of the pain of trauma and addiction and the power of healing and recovery.

Sandi Klein, my longtime assistant, who kept me together through this writing process and has been there for both the conception and delivery of another one of my books. Your feedback was invaluable.

Scott Edelstein, for helping organize the framework of the manuscript and contributing breadth and depth to the understanding of trauma and addiction within families.

The Central Recovery Press team, Nancy Schenck, and Patrick Hughes, for their insights and support.

INTRODUCTION

No one deserves to live a life filled with fear and shame. And no one should have to. Yet, sadly, for most people whose lives have been affected by trauma and addiction, fear and shame are near-constant companions. But they do not have to be. It is possible to heal and recover.

You do not have to live a fear-driven life. You do not have to feel overwhelmed or hypervigilant. You don't have to be afraid of experiencing your emotions or of what they might do to you or others. You don't have to feel anxious or depressed or rageful or spiteful or numb or frozen in place. These emotions are not your destiny.

You deserve to join the ranks of people whose lives are no longer based in fear and shame, who no longer follow toxic internal scripts that have been passed down from generation to generation. You deserve to live a life based on your own goals, values, and choices.

You can learn how to trust, how to set effective limits with others, how to value your own needs, and how to advocate for your needs. You can build a stronger sense of self and personal integrity. You can have a more hopeful, resilient, and joyful future. You can put the past behind you so that it no longer dictates how you live your life today.

You will do this not by ignoring or denying what has happened to you, but by exploring it, moving through and beyond it, and creating a new narrative.

I know this is possible, because in my work as a therapist I have watched as people of all ages moved from despair to hope, from self-doubt to confidence, from confusion to clarity, from anxiety to serenity, from bondage to freedom, and from misery to happiness, and even joy.

Having been raised with addiction, violence, and trauma, I know what it means to live in a chronic state of fear and the sadness of how that can destroy people's lives. Today I also know that recovery is possible. It begins when you reach out for help.

Trauma, Addiction, and You

In my forty-plus years as a therapist, I have discovered that the combination of trauma and addiction is the single greatest cause of dysfunction in families—and one of the most potent negative forces in people's lives.

Until recently, not much was known about the often powerful, often subtle interplay of trauma and addiction. Visit an online bookstore and you can easily find books on addiction and on trauma. But little is available on the interaction of the two and on how that interaction profoundly harms human beings. There is even less available on the process of recovering and healing from their combined effects. I wrote this book to fill that gap.

This book is for anyone whose life has been harmed by the twin forces of trauma and addiction. No matter how much or how little you have already healed—this book can provide you with skills, tools, support, understanding, information, new perspectives, and encouragement.

If you're just beginning to recognize how trauma and addiction influence who you are today, you will find a great deal of help here. If you're already well into your own healing and recovery, but feel some pieces are still missing, this book has much to offer you as well.

Whether you are still in active addiction or have been in recovery for decades, or if you have never directly suffered from addiction but have been harmed by the addictive behavior of others, you will find insight and hope.

This book is not about finding an excuse for your problems. It is about recognizing what lies behind many of those problems, living a process of healing and recovery, and creating a freer, happier life.

The Human Connection

While this book is an indispensable companion for your healing and recovery, it is not the only resource you will need. There is no substitute for the help of caring human beings. You, I, and everyone else need such people in our lives. In your healing from trauma and addiction, these people will likely include at least one professional, such as a psychologist or clinical social worker. It may involve at least one spiritual leader. It will probably involve one or more trusted friends. If you are fortunate, it may also involve trusted family members.

Finding and connecting with caring, trustworthy people will become a key part of your healing.

The Thread of Trauma and Addiction over the Years

During my time working with others, I've been privileged to witness the transformation of thousands of people's lives and watched with awe and appreciation as they developed direction, hope, and self-confidence.

I have spent my career helping people to recover from addiction; to heal from trauma, depression, and anxieties; to let go of self-defeating behaviors and beliefs; to end or heal painful relationships; and to create new ways of being and relating to others.

I began by working in residential programs for teenage girls from highly dysfunctional, addictive families. Then I worked for a rape prevention organization, where I helped women learn to trust their instincts and become more assertive at a time of vulnerability, making it more likely they could move to safety or elicit help.

While in graduate school I worked as an intern in the physical rehabilitation unit of a city hospital with patients who had been seriously injured in traumatic events. Often alcohol or other drugs were involved. In many cases, family members were unable to respond in helpful ways because of their own addiction. Later, I created the first therapy groups for children—from pre-adolescents to young adults—who grew up in alcoholic family systems. I then began my work in inpatient addiction programs where generational repetition was quickly apparent.

Over the years, in these very different jobs, I began to recognize a common thread: the intersection of trauma and addiction. I saw how this interplay repeatedly created self-defeating actions and unhealthy relationships. I also saw how addiction—substance and behavioral—often gets passed on from person to person and from generation to generation. And I saw how depression, anxiety, secrets, and shame were all-too-common parts of this toxic legacy.

However, only recently have therapists developed a common language for talking about trauma. Furthermore, until the beginning of the twenty-first century, very few of us specialized in the healing of trauma.

At roughly the same time, it became clear that traditional talk therapies were not enough to help people heal from trauma. Clinicians were recognizing the importance and great value of experiential therapies, action-based therapies, mindfulness practices, body-mind connection therapies, imagery and visualization, journaling, and expressive arts. We also realized that people who had suffered trauma needed greater emotional safety than we therapists typically provided.

As the understanding and treatment of trauma improved, so did the ways in which clinicians approached addiction. For example, for some years, addiction treatment professionals had worked to help people understand how addiction is typically a family disease; how family members often enabled addiction; and how to put a stop to that enabling. Yet, for years, our efforts at reducing codependence and enabling yielded only modest results. Eventually, we came to understand there were usually underlying trauma issues involved. These created a fear of conflict, a fear of rejection, and a need for approval in family members. These trauma issues sabotaged people's ability to care for themselves, set effective boundaries, and hold addicts accountable for their actions.

As the years passed and I worked with hundreds of addicts of all kinds, I came to recognize how the common, co-occurring issues of depression, anxiety, relapse, and self-defeating relationships were often related to underlying trauma. I also learned that, unless this trauma was healed, long-term recovery would be difficult if not impossible for many people to maintain.

I also began to understand how being raised in an addictive environment often has delayed effects. People may appear to be quite resilient and appear to be doing well during their growing up years, only to have in adulthood severe relational, emotional, mental health, and addiction issues arise seemingly out of nowhere. We now know these are often delayed trauma responses to the deep, chronic stressors that occurred as a result from growing up with addiction.

Since the late 1990s I have been a Senior Fellow at The Meadows, a psychiatric facility in Arizona that specializes in treating the combination of trauma and addiction. Today I work mostly in The Meadows' young adult program, where I am the clinical architect of its Claudia Black Young Adult Center. The young people I work with are just a few years older than the adolescents I began my career working with in the 1970s. Yet their issues are the same: depression, self-loathing, anxiety, self-harm, and addictive behavior.

Today, however, our knowledge of addiction, trauma, and their interaction is far more vast than it was even a few years ago. Neuroscience has validated much of what we suspected about how addiction and trauma affect various parts of the brain. We also understand just how complex trauma, addiction, and their interaction can be. Most notably, we can now offer a far greater range of effective resources and therapy.

An Invitation

I have enormous respect for anyone who sets aside denial, acknowledges his or her past, and moves into and through the emotional pain of healing. I invite you to join this group of courageous human beings who have chosen lives of transformation.

It is my honor to assist you in your recovery and healing, and to walk parts of the journey with you as you create a new narrative for your life and live into a future of hope, happiness, and freedom.

AUTHOR'S NOTE

All names have been changed to honor anonymity in the examples and stories used throughout this book.

I strongly encourage the reader to keep a journal or notebook at hand so as to be able to respond to the exercises presented in various chapters. I also suggest you use a highlighter to emphasize the messages and words that speak to you. This allows you to readily find the information that was significant to your life.

I speak to you very personally, so throughout your reading be cognizant of your breathing, pause, and take deep breaths to stay grounded and to be able to hear the message.

To help with this you will see the icon suggesting a pause.

CHAPTER ONE

Getting to Know Trauma

The word *trauma* conjures up a mental picture of a natural disaster, an armed robbery, or a terrorist attack. But for people in an addicted family, the hurricane is in their home; the trauma is a part of the workings of their own family system.

Let's meet three people whose lives have been profoundly affected by both trauma and addiction.

Jason, age thirty, is a first responder—an Emergency Medical Technician (EMT) and firefighter. He has spent the last ten years responding to people in crisis. In his fourth year as an EMT, Jason and his team of six became trapped in a burning building. He was the only one who made it out alive. Until that event, Jason was a light drinker. Today, eleven months later, he drinks alcohol every evening, usually until he is drunk.

Jason's father was a successful businessman—and an alcoholic—who was rarely at home. His mother stayed busy trying to maintain order and stability for Jason and his two sisters.

Ashleigh, age thirty-six, is single and self-supporting. She lives a quiet life. She has many acquaintances, but no romantic partner nor close friends. She occasionally speaks to her two sisters by telephone. She has held the same job as a bank teller for the past fourteen years. She has been offered promotions three times, but turned them all down, preferring the security of something she knows and is good at.

From the outside, Ashleigh appears to be introverted, pleasant, and content. What others do not see is Ashleigh's deep-seated resistance to change, as well as her hypervigilance to the first sign of potential danger of any kind—whether physical, emotional, or financial. Ashleigh sometimes perceives danger where none exists, such as when she feels misunderstood, when someone disagrees with her, or when her figures don't add up perfectly at the end of the working day. She is too frightened of intimacy to allow herself a close and loving relationship. She often lies awake at night, listening to noises, and frequently awakens startled and afraid. It sometimes takes her hours to contain her fears and fall back to sleep. Her entire life is structured around her attempts to control her circumstances and feel safe.

Ashleigh was raised by an alcoholic mother who was also addicted to prescription pain pills and a father with borderline personality disorder who often flew into rages, usually without warning. He vented his rage almost always on Ashleigh or her mother.

Jake, age twenty-seven, grew up in a stable working-class home until he entered elementary school. His life suddenly became much more difficult when his father, who worked in a steel mill, was injured on the job and began drinking heavily. He also became addicted to oxycodone. After the injury he had trouble keeping a job, and the family moved every few months. Jake's parents argued regularly.

One night when Jake was twelve, his father drove into a tree. Jake's mother was killed; his father was sent to prison for driving while intoxicated since it was his third drunk driving charge. Jake and his sister had no living relatives, so they were both put into foster care. By the time Jake was fifteen, he was living on the street, where he found a sense of belonging and acceptance.

At age twenty, while high on crystal meth, Jake drove a borrowed car into a culvert. The car turned over, injuring his spine and paralyzing him. Since then he has spent his days in a wheelchair. Recently he was admitted to an addiction treatment center.

Jason, Ashleigh, and Jake all grew up in families that were profoundly affected by addiction. From the outside their lives look completely different, but their interior lives have many similarities. All three suffer from what is called **developmental trauma** (or, sometimes, **complex trauma**). These are forms of trauma that were inflicted on them repeatedly by someone they knew and couldn't avoid.

As these examples illustrate, in families trauma tends to beget trauma: parents who have been traumatized often (but not always) pass on that trauma to their kids. The same is true with addiction. When a parent suffers with the disease of addiction, his or her children frequently struggle with addiction as well.

Trauma and addiction often go together. In fact, the two frequently create a toxic dance, reinforcing each other and then passing themselves down from generation to generation. That's the bad news.

The good news is that recovery is possible. Today, trauma and addiction are both treatable. Because trauma and addiction reinforce one another, it would be most ideal if the two were treated in tandem.

In later chapters I'll discuss in more detail the interplay of addiction and trauma and treatment and recovery implications for both. First, though, it's important for you to have a clear understanding of trauma.

What Is Trauma?

Trauma is a Greek word that means a wound, a hurt, or a defeat. Trauma is not a disease or a condition. It is the body's and the brain's response to a severe, painful experience that overwhelms one's ability to cope with the resulting rush of feelings and thoughts.

This experience doesn't have to be something that makes the news, like an earthquake or car wreck or wild animal attack. It can be the sudden death of a friend or beloved pet; someone discovering his or her spouse has been having an affair; or, for a child, a spanking by an angry parent for some transgression the parent erroneously believed the child committed.

Here are some key aspects of trauma:

- **It is caused by an event that the body and parts of the brain perceive as overwhelming or terrifying.** Trauma is the result of a shock to the body, mind, or soul. It can be caused by any stimulus too powerful or too sudden and unexpected to be assimilated or processed in a normal way.
- **The event behind trauma may or may not be genuinely dangerous.** Trauma can be caused by something small but

startling, such as a firecracker exploding harmlessly at your feet. What makes an event traumatic is not its size or level of actual danger, but your degree of distress in response to that event.

- **Trauma is not the event itself, but your response to that event; this response involves fear, helplessness, horror, shock, or some combination.** A catastrophic or painful event doesn't automatically create trauma. For example, imagine a tornado blows your house to bits while you and your family huddle together in the basement. When the storm passes, everyone is grateful to be alive and unharmed. But each person will have his or her own unique response to the experience. Some family members may be shaken but emotionally intact, while others may suffer serious trauma. The same can be true of two children raised in the same abusive family: one may grow up showing a lot of resilience, while the other may struggle with severe trauma responses.

- **Trauma freezes the moment in time and implants powerful thoughts, emotions, and physical sensations in the body and parts of the brain.** These remain embedded—potentially for years or decades—until the trauma is addressed and healed. Some of the tornado survivors I just wrote about, for example, might never forget the sound of the storm approaching or the sight of the ceiling above them being torn away. Others might panic whenever they stand close to an approaching train because the sound reminds them of the tornado as it bore down on their home.

- **Trauma breaks down your psychological defenses and may shatter your sense of security.** If you experience trauma, from that moment on your view of life may be quite different. This may be situational (for example, if you were sexually abused as a child by a minister, you may feel deeply uneasy whenever you go into a church) or it may be general (you might not feel safe being alone with anyone). Trauma can also change your view of yourself (for example, from someone who is strong and resilient to someone who is frightened and vulnerable). At its worst, trauma can make you feel that the world is inherently dangerous or that no one can be trusted or that there is no hope.

- **As a general rule, if you feel you have some control over what is happening, you're less likely to suffer trauma.** The critical difference between an event that is stressful but manageable and one that becomes traumatic is a sense of helplessness. If you are able to avoid, delay, minimize, or prepare for a painful event—or address it effectively very soon afterward—it's far less likely to create trauma. It's why a painful situation tends to create trauma when you can see it coming but can't do a thing about it. Think of the six-year-old child who gets beaten for no reason by an abusive parent or the adult who looks up milliseconds before a falling brick lands on him or her.

  Of course, sometimes control or helplessness can be in the mind of the beholder. In the case of the tornado survivors, some family members might feel the tornado's destruction was entirely out of their control, which is true. But other family members might think, *Thank God we had the presence of mind to head for the basement. That decision saved our lives.* That's just as true. But the first thought encourages a feeling of helplessness, while the second supports a sense of empowerment.

- **The help that others provide (or fail to provide) soon after a traumatic event can have a profound effect on how well and how quickly you recover.** When you experience a traumatic event, it's natural to ask for help and to attempt to connect with other people. If others respond with empathy, assistance, and caring, then you can quickly begin to heal and start to feel safe in the world. But if others refuse to step in and assist or if they ignore you or blame you for the incident or don't take your pain seriously, then this can be as wounding as the trauma itself. And if you feel so vulnerable and unsafe that you cannot ask anyone for help, this can create secondary traumatic wounds.

- **Most events that cause trauma are unexpected.** You're much more likely to experience trauma when you're unprepared for an event—when a car careens around a corner and hits you, or a man steps out of the shadows and robs you at gunpoint, or the balcony you're standing on suddenly collapses.

- **Trauma can also be the result of a string of expected but unavoidable painful events, repeated over and over.** This trauma is common among children who grow up in dysfunctional families or who fall under the influence of an abusive authority figure. This dynamic was present in the childhoods of Jason, Ashleigh, and Jake: all three grew up with predictable, painful, repetitive events they could do nothing about. At first, they were able to manage their emotional wounds, but over time those wounds became traumatic.

- **Many traumas occur in the context of a relationship.** In these situations, people are hurt repeatedly or unexpectedly by someone they trust or care about.

- **In general, the younger a person who experiences a relational trauma, the greater an impact it will have on his or her life.** In part, this is because we're much more vulnerable when we're young; in part, it's because as we grow up our brains and bodies are still developing and the trauma impinges on that development.

- **Trauma isn't just an individual response. It can also be collective and historical.** Entire groups of people can be traumatized together. Think of Africans who were sold into slavery or Jews who were sent to concentration camps or Native Americans who were murdered or relocated to reservations. Think of the people of New Orleans who survived Hurricane Katrina or the residents of Fukushima, Japan, who survived the 2011 earthquake and tsunami. This collective trauma tends to be passed from one group member to another—and from parent to child, down through the generations.

- **Trauma is common, not rare.** Trauma isn't like a virus, striking only the most vulnerable. Any human being, regardless of his or her age, emotional maturity, or state of health, can experience trauma. In fact, almost all of us hold some trauma in our bodies. Many of these traumas are small, and we create ways to work around them that don't seriously diminish our lives. But many other traumas run quite deep and can cause serious pain.

- **Trauma—even in severe or persistent cases—does not automatically lead to chronic misery or dysfunction.** The effects of trauma differ widely from one person to another. Some people can be astonishingly resilient, withstanding or bouncing back from trauma. Others may not be so resilient or may be more resilient to some types of trauma than others. Looking back at Jason, Jake, and Ashleigh, you may be tempted to make assumptions about who had the most painful past, who has more resilience, and who is most likely to thrive in spite of his or her trauma. But the strengths, vulnerabilities, attitudes, and experiences each human being possesses are unique. And while many of us hold trauma in our bodies, we don't live painful lives. But it's also important to understand that unhealed trauma nevertheless does get in the way of your happiness. Healing that trauma will help you be happier, more serene, and more connected to others.

Big T, Little t

Among clinicians in the field of trauma therapy, traumas are often categorized as Big T Traumas or little t traumas. The events behind Big T Traumas tend to be obvious and acute; those behind little t traumas are typically subtler and chronic. While this language resonates with many trauma survivors, in no way is the term "Big" meant to diminish the impact of those referred to as "little." What was traumatic for you, big or little, is significant.

Big T Traumas result from identifiable events that almost anyone would find disturbing. A Big T Trauma is often the outcome of a single event, such as a train crash; but it can also be the result of a sequence of repeated or ongoing events, such as occupation by foreign troops. Other common examples include:

- War, invasion, attack, violent revolution, an act of terrorism, etc.
- Natural disasters such as floods, fires, hurricanes, landslides, etc.
- Rape
- Sexual or physical abuse
- Violence in the home
- Car, train, plane, or bus accidents
- Crime victimization
- Captivity
- Serious injury or illness
- Acts of racism
- Witnessing violence
- Chronic neglect, especially among children and the elderly
- The unexpected death of someone close to you
- Forced relocation, becoming a refugee, living in an internment camp, etc.

Little t traumas are more subtle, often chronic, and much more common than Big T Traumas. In fact, they are so common that we often don't recognize the effect they can have on us. Little t traumas may be responses to

- Failing at something important to you.
- Losses (the loss of a friend, a prized possession, a hoped-for promotion, etc.).
- High stress at work or school.
- Harsh, unfair, or extreme criticism.
- Rejection.
- Being bullied.
- Being shamed or demeaned.
- Being yelled at.
- Being ignored, disrespected, or discounted.
- Betrayal.
- Control or manipulation by someone you trust, especially an authority figure.
- Discovering or witnessing the infidelity of your partner or parent.

- Inconsistent or contradictory responses from a parent or partner.
- A lack of empathy from a parent or a partner.
- Unrealistic expectations.
- An acrimonious divorce.
- Spiritual boundary violations (for example, if someone uses his or her religious authority to control you or if you're sent for extensive training in a religion you don't believe in).
- Enmeshment (not being allowed to have your own thoughts, feelings, and desires).

As I've noted, trauma is often the result of repetitive, painful events that pile up over time. Some of these events may not become traumatic if they occur only once or even a few times. But they may create cumulative trauma when they are repeated enough times. This means that one person's little t could become another person's Big T.

Each of us has experienced many little t traumas; most of us have also experienced at least one or two Big T Traumas as well. While neither kind of trauma ought to be a part of anyone's typical day, for too many people, traumas are regular occurrences.

Trauma and You

I'd like you to take a few minutes to reflect on the events that may have created traumas in your own life. Bring this book and a notebook or journal along with a pen, pencil, or marker to a quiet place where you can be alone for about thirty minutes.

Get comfortable, and then go back to page 8 and slowly read down the lists of events that can cause Big T and little t traumas. In your notebook or journal, write down each item you have personally experienced. It makes no difference whether the event occurred recently or took place a long time ago or is occurring now.

When you're finished, look back at each of the items you listed, one by one. For each one, spend half a minute or so focusing on how your body feels. If you sense yourself tightening or recoiling, or if some vivid memory or image arises, you've probably touched a place of trauma inside you.

The point of this brief activity is to help you identify the traumas you may have experienced and also to begin to recognize how you carry this trauma in your body.

The Losses of Trauma

Many people who suffer trauma experience a great sense of loss. This might be a loss of:

- **Trust.** You lose faith in a particular person or group, or in human beings in general, or in the whole world.
- **Connection.** You feel distant from a particular person, a certain group, or everyone; you lose the ability to feel close to people you once felt close to.
- **Innocence.** You no longer see the world from a place of wonder, hope, and faith; instead, you carry inside yourself a hard, painful truth about something or someone.
- **Truth or reality.** You're no longer sure what is real or whom to believe.
- **Safety.** You now feel constantly threatened and need to be hypervigilant in order to protect yourself.
- **Sense of self.** You no longer recognize yourself or no longer are clear about who you are or what you value.
- **Boundaries.** You become overly self-protective or overly reactive to others.
- **Orientation in time and space.** You have trouble tracking what day it is or where you are; you may feel less than fully present in your body.
- **Control.** You no longer feel you have much or any influence in the world.
- **Connection to a Higher Power.** You no longer trust that the universe is benevolent or in good hands or that a power greater than yourself is looking after you.
- **Connection to a spiritual tradition or group.** You no longer trust the people, practices, or organization that gave you meaning or comfort in the past.

- **Ability to feel calm or relaxed.** You're generally tense, worried, or afraid.
- **Ability to feel comfortable in your own skin.** Just being who you are, or simply being alive, feels painful or risky.

Trauma can also create a repetitive and profoundly disempowering internal message or belief. This is not necessarily something you verbalize or are even able to verbalize. Instead, it's often a felt (visceral) sense of how things are. This belief or message might focus on yourself, the world, or both. Some common ones include:

- *Nothing in my life will ever improve (or change).*
- *No one can be trusted.*
- *The world is inherently unsafe, and I can't protect myself.*
- *I have no choice (or no good choices).*
- *I'm powerless.*
- *I'm totally stuck.*
- *It's all my fault.*
- *I'm completely, hopelessly screwed up or broken.*
- *I'm unlovable.*
- *I don't deserve anything good (or, nothing good will ever happen to me).*
- *I'm inherently weak.*
- *I'm insignificant (or unimportant).*

Please stop reading for a moment. Go back and reread the above list again. This time, spend a few seconds on each item and pay attention to your body as you read. Do any of the messages sound familiar or feel accurate to you? Write down all the ones that resonate with you.

What Influences Trauma

As previously explained, trauma responses can be unpredictable. There's no way for you to know for certain what events a particular person (including you) will experience as traumatic; how deeply that trauma will become embedded; or how the person will respond when that trauma is triggered. It's like predicting a storm: no one can predict exactly how much rain or snow will fall or exactly when the precipitation will begin and end. Still, it is often possible to make a fairly accurate prediction of tomorrow's weather based on current trends and conditions.

In a similar way, therapists have catalogued some factors that make people more likely, but not certain, to experience trauma. The more prominent these factors are in someone's life, and the more of them that are present, the deeper, longer lasting that trauma is likely to be. Here are examples of these factors:

- **Accumulated stress.** Imagine you have a high-pressure, high-responsibility job that requires frequent travel, which keeps you away from your partner and your young children. Now you learn that your mother has just been diagnosed with Alzheimer's disease.

- **A mental health disorder.** You have struggled with depression for the past several years, just as your father did when he was your age. Then you're involved in a sixteen-car crash on an icy freeway where you witness several people die.

- **Financial instability.** You lost your meaningful and rewarding high-paying job and now must work two jobs to make ends meet. Then you lose your house in a flood.

- **A generally negative or critical outlook on life.** You were raised by an extremely critical single father and life has always felt difficult to you. Now you are married to a hypercritical husband.

- **A lack of emotional resilience.** You don't have strong self-confidence, and you are feeling overworked, underpaid, and unappreciated by your boss. Then she informs everyone on your team that they need to work twelve-hour days for the next month. You freeze and go numb.

- **The severity of the experience that causes the trauma.** A forest fire rages through the woods behind your home. A sudden wind enables the fire to spread to your and your neighbor's houses. You hurry from your burning home, barely saving your life, and watch as it and the one next to it disintegrate before your eyes. When your neighbor returns home from work a few hours later—shortly after the firefighters have left—she discovers that her home, like yours, is a total loss. As traumatic as her loss is she does not have the impact of witnessing the destruction as it was occurring.

- **The source of the trauma.** If you fall down a flight of steps, you'll likely experience both physical and emotional trauma. But if you're deliberately pushed down by a stranger, the emotional trauma will likely be more severe—possibly a Big T Trauma. And if you're deliberately pushed down by your partner or parent or someone else who is supposed to care for you and love you, the betrayal is far more profound, and the trauma will likely be greater.

- **The surprise factor.** If you're bitten by a dog that's been growling at you, you're likely to experience less trauma than if your own normally docile Labrador suddenly bites you as she lies at your feet and you rub her belly. When an event is unexpected or unprecedented, you may be too stunned or confused to protect yourself, wield your power, make a decision, or take positive action. However, the surprise factor isn't usually a part of chronic trauma, because with chronic trauma the painful events are repeated and predictable.

The three most important factors of all, though, are these:

1. **The amount of other traumas you have previously experienced.** Trauma upon trauma has a compounding effect. For example, consider two kids who were raised in the same troubled family. The one who was bullied throughout his school years is likely to have more trauma than the one who wasn't. Or think of two neighbors who huddle together for hours in a storm shelter as a hurricane ravages the neighborhood. The one who experienced years of domestic violence is more apt to experience trauma than the one in a stable and happy relationship. Or consider veterans who return home from foreign conflicts: many experienced terrible things on the battlefield, but those with little prior trauma may move beyond

their PTSD quickly, while those who experienced significant trauma before they were sent overseas may take much longer to recover.

2. **The amount of social support you receive.** Whether that support comes from family, friends, community, or some combination, it can blunt the effects of trauma or make it less likely to occur in the first place. In fact, social support is the single most powerful form of protection against both stress and trauma. This is why when there has been a death or other significant loss in a family, people gather in that family's home. It's why congregations pray together for the healing of individual members who are ill. And it's why people instinctively come together in a crisis.

3. **How old someone is when the event or events occur.** Children are especially susceptible to trauma. Because the event occurred while the child's body, brain, and personality were still being formed—and while the child was developing beliefs about him- or herself, other people, and the world—it may create profound and long-lasting effects.

Paradoxically, though, children—especially very young children—can also survive terrible incidents without serious psychological scars because they don't fully comprehend what is happening. During a disaster or crisis, children look to their parents or other people they trust for guidance or cues on what to do.

Caring adults may lessen the impact when they are calm, protect the children, and/or soothe their immediate fears. For example, during the shootings at Sandy Hook Elementary School, many teachers stayed settled and focused, took charge, gave their students clear instructions, and did their best to protect them. A few even led their kids in singing calming songs.

Childhood Resilience and Vulnerability

Touch is the primary language of childhood. Loving touch between parents and their children provides emotional nourishment and a sense of calm and safety. Most of us know this from our own emotional experience, but there is proven biochemistry behind it as well. Touching your child in a caring way releases oxytocin into both people's bloodstreams. **Oxytocin**, the "bonding hormone," is known for reducing stress, lowering cortisol levels, and increasing a sense of love and security. Touching also floods both people's bodies with **serotonin**, the body's natural antidepressant, which soothes them and regulates their moods. In short, chemicals of connection make us grow up healthy as well as feel good.

There is also proven biochemistry behind stress hormones that make us feel uncomfortable. Our bodies produce these hormones when we're in pain, in danger, or under stress. And, in young people, one of the greatest sources of stress is not being given enough touch, attention, or care. The most notable of these stress hormones is **cortisol**, which floods the brain during stressful events. In infants, cortisol destroys nerve connections in critical portions of the developing brain. We now know that three-month-old infants who are consistently held and cared for produce less cortisol in their brains than infants who receive less-responsive care. Experiments have shown these heightened cortisol levels typically continue for months or years afterward. It appears that the level of stress someone experiences in infancy may shape the stress responses in his or her brain for many years. These responses in turn may affect memory, attention, and emotions throughout his or her life. This is why the experience of trauma at a young age can affect a person negatively for many years to come. It is also why the healing of trauma is so important.

There's another essential aspect to giving kids the care, attention, and loving touch they need. When a child is not adequately cared for, that lack of care tends to make the child more vulnerable to trauma. Children's brains are too immature to manage and regulate themselves in the midst of everyday pressures and stresses. The attention and care provided by caring adults can serve as external sources of regulation. When a caregiver offers safety, comfort, emotional support, and reassurance—commonly expressed through holding, rocking, and caring conversation—the child's neocortex receives this message: *I'm okay; someone is taking care of me.* This helps the child to quickly recover from pain or discomfort. Hurt can quickly turn into playfulness, fear into curiosity, anger into energy, and shame into confidence.

When the attention and care provided are inadequate, however, children recover from pain and discomfort much more slowly. Because they are less resilient and often less physically healthy, they're more likely to experience trauma than children who are better cared for. This limited resiliency also makes it more likely for everyday stresses to compound over time, eventually creating trauma through small but chronic pressures.

The key to avoiding or limiting trauma in your kids is providing them with as many protective experiences as possible. The more of these a child has, the more resilient and less vulnerable to trauma that child is likely to become.

Here are some other experiences that can help children—and adults, too—become more resilient and less vulnerable to trauma:

- A close relationship with at least one caring, nurturing adult (usually but not necessarily a parent)
- A sense of belonging, both at home and in one or more other places (e.g., school, a neighborhood, a religious group or center, an organization such as Little League or Girl Scouts, or the home of a grandparent or other relative)
- Activities outside the home that are easy, safe, lawful, and pleasant (e.g., a chess club, school band, or a writing group)
- A sense of success, achievement, or mastery in at least one activity or aspect of life (e.g., cooking, drawing, dance, basketball, web design, etc.)
- A sense of purpose or meaning in life
- A belief that a positive future lies ahead—or at least is possible

The Biology of Trauma

The human body cannot tell the difference between an emotional emergency and physical danger or, often, between something that's genuinely dangerous and something harmless that's loud, strange, sudden, or unfamiliar. When your body senses danger, whether real or imagined, a part of your brain called the **amygdala** signals it to go on high alert. As a result, all kinds of physical changes occur: your pulse and blood pressure go up; your muscles tense; your pupils get bigger; and your breathing gets shallower.

When your body is triggered by any of these things, it responds by pumping out stress chemicals designed to make you do one of two things: flee for safety or stand and fight. If there is no perceived opportunity to do either one, then your body's automatic response is to make you freeze. Depending on the situation, this might mean standing very still in place, or crawling into bed and refusing to respond to other people, or going numb on the inside. This isn't pathological; it's a survival reflex. Human beings are hardwired to do this.

This freezing can sometimes be an effective survival mechanism. When you are ten years old and your father is raging at you two inches from your face, his face contorted, screaming that you are worthless and stupid, it's not wise to move into fight mode, but nor do you have the ability to flee; so, freezing is your best form of survival in that moment. Most of us have heard that if a bear were to attack you the best thing is to lie on your stomach and be still. If you're immobile, you're less likely to be harmed, thus increasing your eventual opportunities for escape.

And we're not alone. Many animals, from mice to dogs, have the same neurological wiring and respond to perceived threats in the same three ways: by fighting, fleeing, or freezing.

▲▼▲

To better understand the impact of trauma on the human brain, it's helpful to understand some basics of how the brain works. What we call the brain could just as accurately be thought of as three closely connected organs, each with its own separate set of functions. Let's look briefly at each one, starting at the bottom.

The base of the brain connects directly to the spinal cord. It is referred to as the reptilian brain, the lizard brain, or the **R-complex brain**, with *R* standing for *reptilian*. This term *reptilian* refers to our primitive instinctive brain function that is shared by reptiles and mammals including humans. Its number one job is survival as it controls our body's basic functions: reflexive behaviors, balance, breathing, heartbeat, digestion, and so on.

Directly above our reptilian brain is our **limbic brain**, also called the limbic system, the mammalian brain, or the midbrain. We share this part of our brain with all other mammals, from mice to gorillas. The limbic system is the center of all emotion and learning. As it processes sensory input, it instantaneously evaluates everything as either positive or negative. It constantly wants to know the answers to two questions: (1) *Is this safe or dangerous?* and (2) *Is this potentially pleasurable or painful (or comfortable or uncomfortable)?* Our limbic system is designed to help us avoid danger and pain and to repeatedly experience safety and pleasure.

The limbic brain isn't logical. In fact, it has zero capacity to think. Nor does it have a sense of time. To the limbic brain, there is no past or future; everything it experiences, including memories of the past and hopes and fears about the future, takes place right now. The limbic brain contains several structures whose names you don't need to remember, but might hear therapists and neuroscientists mention. These include the amygdala, the thalamus, the hypothalamus, and the hippocampus.

The amygdala's job is to scan all sensory input for any potential threat. It's like a security checkpoint at an airport. If your amygdala identifies something—say, a bowl of soup you pick up—as safe and non-threatening, then it admits the relevant sensory information to the top part of the brain. But if a roach suddenly starts to climb out of the bowl, your amygdala will send an alarm to your thalamus.

The **thalamus** acts as a switchboard. In milliseconds, it redirects that alarm to your reptilian brain in order to respond as quickly as possible to the threat. Your reptilian brain will reflexively make you either fight, flee, or freeze. In a fraction of a second, you'll drop the bowl without knowing why, even before the image of the roach reaches the thinking part of your brain.

Your cognitive experience will be something like this: *Yum, tomato soup. Maybe I should add some—hey, what's going on? Why are my hands pulling apart? I'm dropping the bowl. Oh no—a roach! Ewwww!*

This makes perfect sense from a survival perspective. If you're walking in the desert and are suddenly surprised by a rattlesnake, you'll jump backward before you even consciously see or hear it. That rapid response might save your life.

Now imagine a woman walking down a city street at night. She sees a shadow come up behind her. A moment later, a man grabs her from behind, pulls her into an alley, and tries to rape her. Fortunately, she is able to break free and run away. Years later, as she watches television in her living room, a shadow suddenly appears just outside her window. Without thinking or understanding why, she quickly gets up, runs into her bedroom, and shuts the door. It takes her a few seconds to compose herself and mentally replay the incident. From viewing that replay, she realizes the shadow was a neighborhood teenager retrieving a wayward basketball. She laughs with relief and returns to her living room—but she's still shaking. Her flight response was her reptilian and limbic system at work.

Remember, the limbic brain and reptilian brain don't understand time; they only understand *now*. This is why people with serious trauma can seem stuck in the past; their limbic systems are in charge. To that part of the brain, something that happened fifteen years ago feels as though it is happening right now.

The limbic brain is the center of our emotional life, but its top priority is always survival. So whenever it perceives a threat—regardless of whether the threat is real, misperceived, or completely imaginary—our limbic brain overrides all nonessential functions, including thinking and reasoning, and temporarily puts our reptilian brain in charge. In essence, it briefly hijacks our body for our own protection.

It is believed the limbic brain does not become fully functional in human beings until the ages of four to five. Because of their partially undeveloped limbic system, young children often don't have the capacity to understand what is happening or to regulate their emotional responses. This is why kids sometimes get so excited or so scared. They depend on the adults around them to help them contain their excitement or soothe their intense fear.

Now let's look at the biggest part of your brain. Directly above and largely surrounding your limbic brain is your thinking brain—also known as the **cerebral brain**—cerebrum, neocortex, prefrontal cortex (PFC), cortex, cognitive brain, or executive brain. This is the part of your brain that analyzes, organizes, plans, anticipates, imagines, thinks logically, and understands. It enables you to listen, to suspend judgment, to have empathy, to mediate, to negotiate, and to create a story out of events.

The **neocortex** is also in charge of impulse control. If you want to call your boss a jerk to his face, your neocortex is the part of your brain that sees the likely consequences of that action and makes you hold your tongue. The neocortex does not become fully formed until our early to mid-twenties. This is why teenagers often act impulsively and don't think logically. Their brains aren't yet fully formed. This is partly why it's so important for teenagers and children to have healthy adults in their lives who can guide them, mentor them, and help them solve problems.

Most people don't understand that when a trauma-inducing incident occurs and the limbic and reptilian brains are activated, the neocortex gets completely bypassed. It is literally not involved in the event. This makes sense from a survival perspective. If you see a tiger running toward you, you need to instantly run, or throw a rock or shoot a gun at it, or fall down and play dead. You can't reason your way out of a tiger attack.

This has profound implications for how trauma needs to be healed. Because the neocortex is uninvolved in the creation of trauma, you can't heal trauma through reason or cognitive examination or traditional talk therapy alone. The thinking brain is the wrong tool for the job.

Imagine you fall off a wall and land hard on your back. The limbic and reptilian parts of your brain may register the event as trauma. But the wall is only three feet tall, so you're shaken up but physically unharmed. Your neocortex gets over the event and has forgotten about it within five minutes. But it's a completely different story for your limbic and reptilian brains. To them, the trauma may be real, painful, frightening, and happening right now. You can tell yourself over and over, *It was just a short fall, and I got right up and walked away,* but this won't help at all. In order to heal, you'll need to address the trauma in these non-thinking parts of your brain.

Trauma and the Nervous System

Repetitive stressors don't just affect children; they are part of life for every human being. You're intimately familiar with hundreds of these: overwork, family demands, noise pollution, long commutes, annoying in-laws, overly loud music, terrorism reported on the evening news, junk phone calls, and so on.

The best defense against all these stressors is a well-regulated nervous system. This means being able to soothe and calm yourself down in the face of conflict, pain, or discomfort. For example, you might want to curse at the texting woman who walks into you on the sidewalk. But if your nervous system is properly regulated, you'll instead touch her arm and say, "Excuse me, watch where you're going or you'll hurt someone, okay?" A well-regulated nervous system also means being able to get up in the morning and go to work, even though you'd rather stay in bed.

Most of us don't routinely experience extreme highs or lows in our energy and emotions. We do experience them, but only in situations of high stress, danger, or excitement. That's one result of a well-regulated nervous system.

Another result is a sense of well-being—a feeling that things are basically okay, even if you're facing pain or problems.

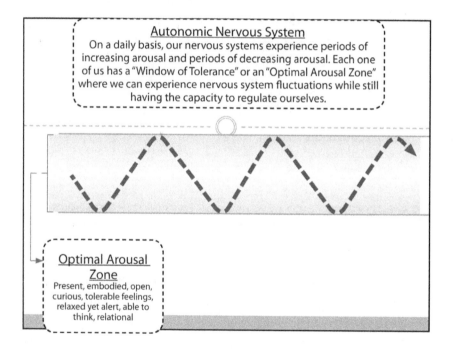

Autonomic Nervous System
On a daily basis, our nervous systems experience periods of increasing arousal and periods of decreasing arousal. Each one of us has a "Window of Tolerance" or an "Optimal Arousal Zone" where we can experience nervous system fluctuations while still having the capacity to regulate ourselves.

Optimal Arousal Zone
Present, embodied, open, curious, tolerable feelings, relaxed yet alert, able to think, relational

People with trauma—especially serious trauma—tend to have poorly regulated nervous systems. Instead of staying within a relatively comfortable and comforting range, they tend to over-activate or under-activate, and the person easily becomes excited, agitated, anxious, tired, defeated, or depressed. They also tend to move into fight, flight, or freeze mode more easily. People whose nervous systems are poorly regulated may also experience anxiety, panic, difficulty relaxing, restlessness, difficulty sleeping, hostility, chronic low energy, or other such symptoms.

It's common for someone who stays in an over- or under-activated state for weeks or months to get stuck there. In clinical language, we say the dysregulation becomes chronic. This is precisely what happens to many people with unhealed trauma.

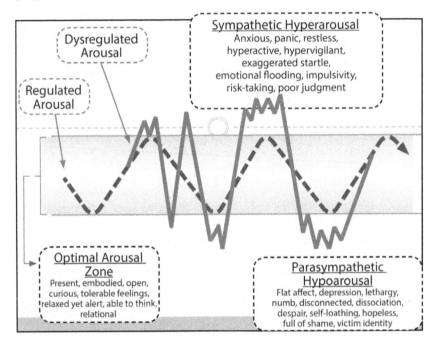

As you'll see in later chapters, people who live with trauma often attempt to blunt the resulting pain or discomfort with drugs, alcohol, shopping, gambling, intense work, sex, online gaming, the binge-watching of videos, or other activities that can become addictive.

No one is free of trauma. Yet trauma is not a prison sentence. It is not something we are forced to endure or work around. Trauma can be healed.

CHAPTER TWO

What We Know About Addiction

Ask a hundred people what addiction is and you'll get a hundred different answers. But ask those same hundred people how addiction impacts a family and you'll get much more consensus. Addiction harms every family it touches—and destroys some of them.

Because most people can choose to drink or not drink alcohol, many still blame alcoholics for their addiction. Similarly, because many people enjoy gambling and can stop whenever they please, those people incorrectly assume the cause of gambling addiction is the addict's weak will. And because most of us in committed relationships may feel physically attracted to another person but don't act on that attraction, we assume people with sex addiction are simply too selfish or thoughtless to exercise the same restraint. These beliefs simply do not reflect the realities of addiction.

No one wants to become addicted. Those who suffer with the disease of addiction may want to obliterate their pain, escape from the world, lessen their stress, or be part of a particular social group. But no one thinks, *I want to lose all control over my behavior. I want to drink, use, gamble, binge, shop, work, etc. to the point I lose my friends, my family, my health, and my job.*

This loss of control is the central characteristic of addiction. The addict loses control over his or her ability to say no to a drink, a bet, a bargain, a doughnut, or a hookup with a stranger.

Why do some people become addicted and others do not? The answer is complex. Some people are genetically predisposed to addiction, but researchers are quick to say that a predisposition is not fate or predestination. It just means there is a higher probability that addiction may activate under the right or, more accurately, the wrong circumstances.

A variety of environmental factors can also predispose some people to addiction. These include family modeling (we tend to do what our family members do); peer influences (we tend to do what our peers do); and cultural reinforcement (we tend to do what society and respected institutions want us to do).

Trauma, too, predisposes people to addiction. In fact, childhood trauma is the single greatest contributor to such a predisposition. A child who is abused or abandoned or who suffers a major loss, such as the death of a sibling or the acrimonious divorce of his or her parents, tends to become much more vulnerable to addiction. Furthermore, anyone, at any age, may become more vulnerable to addiction if that person suffers a serious accident or injury, a chronic illness, the death of a family member, or the sudden loss of a job, a home, or a close relationship. Addiction also shows up more often in people who have been victims of serious crimes (rape, assault, torture, etc.) or who have personally endured or witnessed acts of war or terrorism.

A genetic disposition coupled with any psychological injury is a setup for addiction.

Addiction's Two Faces

There are two general types of addiction:

- **Substance addiction** is the compulsive use of specific drugs, such as alcohol, heroin, opiates/opioids, caffeine, nicotine, etc. This compulsive use causes changes in the body's and brain's biochemistry that are directly created by the ingestion of one of these substances.

- **Process addiction** (also called **behavioral addiction**) involves similar changes to the brain's biochemistry, but no ingestion of an addictive substance. Instead, a process addiction involves a compulsion to repeat an activity, such as gambling, shopping, online gaming, using social media, sex, exercise, overworking, binge eating and purging, or calorie restriction. For some people, even a romantic relationship or the use of anything with a screen (a smartphone, a computer, a gaming console) can become addictive and lead to addiction.

From the brain's viewpoint, substance and process addiction are identical. As Jason Z. W. Powers, MD, observes in his book *When the Servant Becomes the Master*, "As far as the brain is concerned, a reward is a reward, regardless of whether it comes from a substance, behavior, or experience."

Addiction is an equal-opportunity illness. It affects over twenty-three million people in America alone, regardless of their economic status, political views, gender, sexual orientation, intellectual abilities, schooling, worldly achievements, religion, race, ethnicity, or beliefs. Addicts are factory workers, inventors, clergy, sales people, janitors, policemen, accountants, physicians, politicians, executives, and homemakers.

Addiction is never about a particular behavior or substance—what someone does or uses. It's about the continued practice of an activity or the continued use of a substance despite painful consequences that significantly interfere with the person's life.

Lots of people drink alcohol, but there is a profound, essential difference between the social drinker and the alcoholic. Plenty of people gamble, but fewer are gambling addicts. Many people have casual sex, but a sex addict may look for a different sexual partner each night, even when his or her marriage and family are at stake.

The Signs of Addiction

Like most other diseases, untreated addiction follows a predictable and reproducible pattern. All manifestations or forms of addiction follow the same trajectory—and the same cycle of pain. In the **learning phase**, a person discovers that he feels good whenever he uses a substance (e.g., alcohol, oxycodone, crystal meth, etc.) or engages in an activity (e.g., gamble, play online games, view porn and masturbate). In this early stage, there are usually few or no serious negative consequences. This often gives the person a false sense of power, confidence, and relief from pain.

Pain Cycle

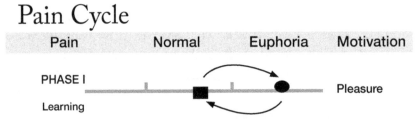

Graph adapted from Vernon Johnson, MD.

Once the person has used the substance or performed the activity enough times, he then enters the **seeking phase**. He spends more and more time seeking, planning, arranging, and experiencing the addictive behavior or the use of the addictive substance. He discovers that he now needs more and more of the substance or activity to create the same good feelings. He begins to seek this mood change regularly, trying to recapture the euphoria of his earlier positive experiences. In the seeking phase, the person no longer seeks pleasure so much as relief.

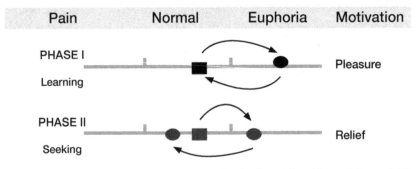

Graph adapted from Vernon Johnson, MD.

If the person continues the activity or substance use, he eventually enters the **dependency phase**. This is where serious physical, emotional, and often financial consequences begin to arise. The person needs progressively more and more of the substance or more and more repetitions of the behavior to get relief. He also spends more time recovering from the highs and lows that are invariably involved. Meanwhile, his ordinary state becomes increasingly unstable and painful. He no longer seeks pleasure or even relief; he is simply trying to keep his life from collapsing. Meanwhile, he feels an increasing loss of control over his ability to think, reason, and make choices or decisions, especially in relation to his addiction. His self-worth deteriorates. So do his relationships with others.

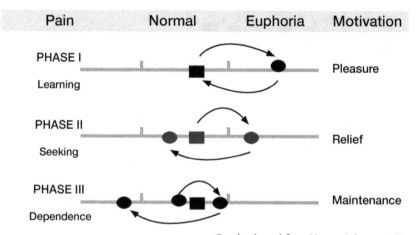

Graph adapted from Vernon Johnson, MD.

If the person continues in this downward spiral, he then enters the **chronic dependence phase**. In this phase, the person is in pain much of the time. His family and social relationships deteriorate badly. His body responds to the damage done to it with illness, exhaustion, or both. His finances suffer.

Most notably, the addictive behavior is no longer a means of feeling good. It is merely a way to blunt the pain and get through the day. The person's primary motivation is now *escape*—from the pain he feels, the pain he causes others, and the chronic mess his life has become. Eventually, if addiction is not treated, the addict usually ends up incarcerated, in a psychiatric facility, or dead.

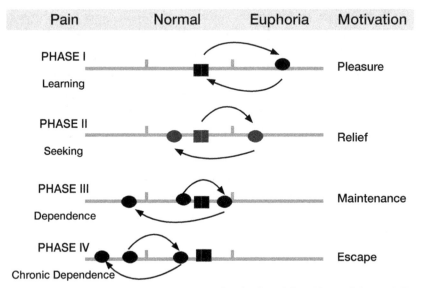

Graph adapted from Vernon Johnson, MD.

A handful of key elements define addiction and all of its manifestations. These include:

- The compulsive nature of the activity (shopping, drinking, snorting cocaine, working, using the internet, viewing porn, gambling, etc.)
- The regular repetition of the activity, despite its negative consequences
- A gradually increasing need for more and more of the activity or substance to achieve results (pleasure, relief, stability, or escape)
- Emotional, and often physical, pain
- The persistent pursuit of self-destructive or high-risk behavior, in which the person sacrifices previously cherished aspects of his or her life (rewarding relationships, self-worth, career success, etc.)
- An increasing loss of control over his or her behavior and life

Once the illness of addiction takes hold, the addict typically denies, ignores, or doesn't see the problems created by his or her compulsive behavior. Instead, the addict rationalizes that behavior:

- "It's only one bottle of gin a day. That's not a lot."
- "So what if I'm up all night gaming? So is almost everyone else on the site."
- "How can I have a shopping problem? My partner makes $200,000 a year. We can afford it."
- "I'm stuck at home with all these kids while you have a life. Food is my only comfort."
- "I'm not the one with the sex problem. You are, with your prudish Victorian morality."

In the early stages of addiction, an addict usually establishes a set of internal rules that allows him or her to believe—or pretend—he or she has control over his or her behavior. For example:

- "I never take a drink before noon."
- "I only do coke when I don't have school the next day."
- "Once I get down to ninety pounds, I'll be thin enough, and I'll stop vomiting."
- "I take sixty dollars into the casino with me each day. Once it's gone—or once I win $200—I leave. No 'ifs, ands, or buts.' I might stay to watch or have something to eat, but no more gambling that day."

These restrictions help addicts believe—incorrectly—they can limit or stop the addictive activity at any time. But as addiction progresses, they eventually begin to break their own rules. That's when the downward spiral starts to seriously worsen, unless it is disrupted with a program of recovery.

As addicts become increasingly preoccupied with their addiction, their thinking becomes steadily more distorted. They defend and justify their behavior ever more vigorously, dodge all responsibility for their actions, and blame and attack others. They retreat further and further from friends, family, work, and reality in general. They take bigger and bigger risks. Eventually those risks cause them to crash and burn.

Addiction and the Brain

I define *addiction* as *a pathological relationship with one or more mood-altering chemicals.*

This chemical may be a substance that a person puts into her body. Or it may be a chemical released in her brain when she repeats a certain activity, such as smoking meth, playing poker, exercising strenuously, or engaging in online porn. Either way, having that chemical in her brain eventually becomes more important to her than her relationships, her health, or her work. The presence of this chemical also becomes necessary for the person to simply feel normal—even as her life has become anything but normal. Because that chemical becomes central to the person's life and sense of normalcy, any vow to stop the addictive activity gets lost in the shadow of active addiction.

Both substance and/or process addiction involve the same natural neurochemicals. Furthermore, process addiction stimulates and rewards the same neural pathways in the brain as substance addiction. When the addict engages in the compulsive activity or ingests the addictive substance, it causes dopamine, adrenaline, endorphins, and serotonin to be released into his or her brain's limbic system. In fact, we now know that some of these chemicals are released just before the activity or ingestion occurs in anticipation of the reward.

Dopamine and adrenaline trigger the brain's pleasure/reward center; serotonin lessens anxiety and depression; endorphins do both and reduce pain as well. These are all part of our natural system of neurotransmitters and painkillers.

These neurochemicals have one other attribute: They increase our ability to later recall how great we felt. This encourages us to repeat the same experience again and again and again. This, in a nutshell, is how the disease of addiction operates.

Adopted in 2011 by the American Society of Addiction Medicine (ASAM), *addiction* is defined as

> a primary, chronic disease of brain reward, motivation, memory and related circuitry. Dysfunction in these circuits leads to characteristic biological, psychological, social, and spiritual manifestations. This is reflected in an

individual pathologically pursuing reward and/or relief by substance use and other behaviors.

Addiction is characterized by inability to consistently abstain, impairment in behavior control, cravings, diminished recognition of significant problems with one's behaviors and interpersonal relationships, and a dysfunctional emotional response. Like other chronic diseases, addiction often involves cycles of relapse and remission. Without treatment or engagement in recovery activities, addiction is progressive and can result in disability or premature death.

Becoming addicted and progressing through the four stages of addiction previously described takes time. But when does a certain repeated activity turn into addiction? At what point does the illness commandeer the brain?

We don't know, and it's possible we never will. There may be no clear, observable, and identifiable threshold. It may be like asking, "At what point does a tadpole become a frog?"

However, as the disease of addiction develops, there does appear to be a tipping point the person with the illness crosses. On one side of the line is the ability to choose to stop; on the other side, all choice is eliminated and all control disappears. The person can no longer stop, change, or heal through willpower alone. The person needs a program of recovery.

Have you ever wanted to ask an addict, "How can you do this? What are you thinking?"

The answer is that people with the disease of addiction literally aren't thinking. Because of their disease, they genuinely cannot think straight—or at all—about what they are doing or the effects their actions have on other people. Either they have become blind to these effects or they have ceased to care.

As one client shared: "My wife stood in front of me, holding the hands of our two- and four-year-old boys, and said I needed to choose between them and my drinking. I didn't waste any time. I said goodbye."

An addict's inability to recognize how his actions harm others—and himself—appears to be connected to brain chemistry. When someone repeats an addictive activity enough times, his brain's reward center starts overriding the cognitive, rational part of the brain.

This is neuroscience, not speculation. Addiction is not so much about a specific substance or activity as it is about disrupting the normal processing of pleasure and the usual process of thinking. Brain scans of addicts show reduced levels of activation in the prefrontal cortex. You'll recall this is the part of the brain where rational thought normally overrides impulsive behavior. In short, the thinking brain is hijacked by addiction. Instead of recognizing long-term consequences, the brain just says to itself, "This feels good; let's do it again."

Being addicted means literally losing your ability to say no to your impulses. A neurochemical balance point shifts, so that the addict experiences more and more (and stronger and stronger) urges and keeps wanting more and more. Meanwhile, the payoff from the addictive activity becomes steadily smaller and smaller—and the addict becomes less and less able to restrain his or her impulses and cravings. This has nothing to do with morality or willpower or strength of character. It has everything to do with the neurochemistry of the brain.

There's a secondary neurological effect as well. When we're under stress—especially extreme stress—the parts of the brain that help us solve problems may shut down, further fueling impulsive behavior. And if there's one thing addiction creates, it's stress.

Addiction doesn't involve lack of self-control or empathy or morality or values or common sense. Nobody knows better than those who grew up with addiction how damaging it becomes. Yet they are the most high-risk group to become addicted. They routinely swear to themselves, *It will never happen to me*. And they mean it with all their heart. They know all too well the destruction addiction can create and how deeply it can wound people. "I will not betray my wife as my father did." "I will not end up alcoholic, like my sister." "I will never hurt my kids physically, the way my mother hurt us."

Let's look more closely at how addiction affects each part of the brain.

As previously mentioned, the thinking brain is called the **prefrontal cortex**, or PFC. This is where we make choices, maintain our values, and follow our own code of ethics. It is the most evolved part of the human brain. Neuroscientists call the prefrontal cortex the brain's executive function—its CEO. Addiction largely shuts down this part of the brain.

The primary part of the brain where addiction thrives is known as the **mesolimbic dopamine system,** or MDS. Located within the limbic system, the MDS is our pleasure and survival center. It is connected to the prefrontal cortex by many highways of neurons.

Addiction redirects the addict's consciousness from the PFC, down these neural highways, and into the MDS. It focuses the person's attention away from thought and toward his or her strongest momentary impulse.

Let's imagine you're six months into recovery from a heroin addiction. You go to a film, and in one scene you see a group of young, sexy people getting high. On your way home on the subway, you find yourself going through your phone looking at pictures of you and some of your former friends partying together and getting loaded. That's your MDS talking.

An instant later, another voice—your prefrontal cortex—says, "Wait a minute. Bad idea. Don't give up what you've gotten in recovery." So you close your browser, plug in your ear buds, and listen to some music instead.

Now imagine what you might have done if your prefrontal cortex hadn't participated in that internal conversation.

All this can sound pretty grim. But neuroscience also gives us some very good news: the human brain—even an addicted brain—has great plasticity to it. The practices addicts can learn in treatment and recovery can positively affect their brain function. They can learn skills that calm the emotionally reactive area of their brain. They can learn to avoid triggers that activate that area. And they can learn to strengthen their prefrontal cortex, so they can rationally think through their decisions and, when necessary, override potentially harmful impulses, like the impulse to call a former dealer and place an order or the impulse to approach the prostitute on the street corner.

Where Trauma and Addiction Meet

Let's look at the question of why people become addicts from another angle. One piece of the answer is simple: all addictive behavior feels good at first. That's why people drink, use drugs, shop until they drop, or look for hookups online. They're not masochists. They're seeking pleasure, like all normal human beings. But at a certain point, the pleasurable experience stops being so pleasurable. Why, then, does the addict keep repeating an activity that has lost its sparkle?

As I noted earlier, in some people it's simply their genetic predisposition for addiction. But there are many other reasons as well. The drug or behavior may:

- Help the addict anesthetize the helplessness, despair, shame, loneliness, confusion, fear, or other inner pain he or she may feel
- Give the addict a false sense of power, control, ability, or self-esteem
- Enable the addict to loosen up and temporarily forget his or her worries and troubles
- Allow the addict to briefly drop out or escape his or her regular life
- Be presented or advertised as cool, sophisticated, mature, or fun
- Be associated with wealth, status, or sexual attractiveness
- Be something done regularly by people they respect, admire, or want to be like
- Help the addict connect with some of these people

It's easy to see how the first four motives connect trauma and addiction. In fact, in the learning phase of addiction, substance use or a compulsive activity can feel like the perfect solution to unhealed trauma. Unfortunately, over time the addict discovers that what feels like a solution is actually the beginning of a very serious problem.

Let's listen to some addicts describe the forces that first pulled them into addiction:

Kylie: "I started out being my dad's best bartender when I was nine, and by the time I was fourteen I was his best drinking and using buddy."

Nicholas: "The only time my father ever acted like he liked me was when he would take me to the races with him."

Pedro: "When I was eleven I took my first drink. I hated the taste, but I felt the glow. It worked. I would get sick as a dog, and then swear on a stack of Bibles that I would stop. But I would still do it again. I got drunk and then, in time, loaded because I had a hole in my gut so big, and when I drank that first time it filled it up. It was the solution. It worked. That was all I knew."

Jack: "There was one reason I ever ingested alcohol, and that was to get blithering numb. Eventually, after deciding alcohol was uncool since that's what our parents did, I started taking drugs. I would take anything to not feel. I didn't feel so scared; life was not so intense. Drugs helped me feel a part of my group of user friends. I looked up to those people. I wanted to be like them."

Dana: "When I did coke, I had no fear. I could fight with whoever got in my way."

Hunter: "I drank to relax. I was so uptight, always needing to be hypervigilant. I drank to relieve the pain. I drank to hide and to mask the way I felt. I was so anxious all of the time. I knew I was screwing up, but I didn't know what else to do."

Hannah: "After being in so many foster homes and after suffering sexual abuse at the hands of one of my foster parents, I wanted to die or, at the very least, disappear. The one source of power I was able to find was in my relationship to food. Restricting my calorie intake enabled me to wield power and control over food. At the same time, by losing weight, I was able to slowly disappear."

Chris: "My father raged and was abusive. By age eleven, I found what my father had—power in his raging. It protected me from my fears, my sense of unworthiness. Rage gave me the high, the power—and masturbation was my anesthetic. They worked in tandem for years."

Each manifestation of addiction offers its own unique way of hooking people. Food offers solace to a child who is hungry for love or attention or to anyone who feels isolated and alone. Starving can be a way to become less and less visible in an attempt to hide from deep inner pain. Cocaine can make someone who usually feels helpless, powerless, and talentless feel powerful and capable instead. Marijuana can help a chronically anxious person relax and feel comfortable.

When Various Forms of Addiction Interact

Here's something few people realize: *most people with addiction are addicted to more than one substance and/or behavior.* Remember, the disease of addiction is not about a particular substance or activity. It is about the brain's response to a substance or activity, and the illness of addiction can make use of a variety of objects.

Most practicing addicts adapt to whatever addictive substance or activity is available. One addict told me, "As each of my fixes failed, I would look for another one. I was looking for that thing that was going to make me okay."

It's quite common to be addicted to multiple substances and/or behaviors at once. And the more unhealed trauma someone has, the more likely he or she is to have multiple manifestations of addiction.

This can happen in a number of possible ways. Some people have several forms of addiction that operate simultaneously. Others trade off by giving up one only to get lost in another. Still others routinely alternate between two or more different substances or activities. Sometimes, when one person has multiple manifestations of addiction (e.g., using alcohol and opiates and gambling) and then becomes abstinent from one of them, the other manifestations grow stronger.

Harry, who is an alcoholic, often gorges himself on ice cream and pizza when he has no access to alcohol.

Brittany has three years of abstinence from heroin, but soon after she got into recovery, she began spending more and more time online and now spends all her free time on social media.

Emma is normally very proper and buttoned up. But when she drinks, she drops her inhibitions, looks for hookups, and engages in online pornography.

When Riaz does cocaine, he feels strong, powerful, and like a winner, so he heads for the racetrack.

Kelly, who receives treatment for her meth addiction and her anorexia, soon finds her sexual compulsive behaviors are escalating.

Eric starts almost every evening by drinking a double espresso, smoking a fat joint, and downing five or six shots of whiskey. He calls this "my triple B cure: buzz, blunt, and booze."

Addicts typically seek help for the manifestation that is strongest, most disruptive, or most visible to others—or the one they have the least shame about. Meanwhile, they may not address or even let on about their other substance use or addictive behaviors. For example, they might go to rehab for their alcohol abuse but try to keep their obsessive use of porn secret, or they seek help for their compulsive shopping but keep popping pain pills.

Addiction often exists in layers, with some forms more deeply embedded than others. Often the various forms of addiction closely interact. For example, someone might combine speed or other amphetamines with sex in an attempt to get a greater high. Or he might use alcohol or marijuana to bring himself down from the previous high.

Sometimes substances and activities are used together in a ritualized way. For example, an addict might use cocaine to build up the courage to pick up a prostitute at a bar. Or she might spend the evening at the mall bingeing on bar food, vomiting in the restroom, and then shopping for three hours.

As one client so eloquently said, "I am addicted to so many things; I am an addiction binger and trader."

Addiction as a Family Disease

Addiction doesn't just belong to the addict; it belongs to the family. Not only does the disease live inside the addict's brain, but it also produces strong symptoms in the brains of the addict's family members, distorting their thinking as much as it distorts the addict's.

The things an addict does—such as dodge responsibility, lie, blame others, and live a double life—are typically the very same things their family members routinely do, whether or not they suffer with addiction. This is particularly true of denial in all its forms, including rationalizing, minimizing, and looking the other way.

As someone slides into addiction, it begins to disrupt his or her daily life, change his or her temperament, and impair his or her thinking and communication. Meanwhile, the addict's family often undergoes a parallel slide into denial. They make excuses for the addict. They tell themselves, each other, and concerned outsiders, "Oh, she works such long hours, she deserves a good night out." Or "He's the sole breadwinner in the family. I really shouldn't complain about his wanting to spend time drinking with his friends." Or "He's not as bad as my dad was." Or "She's got a good heart. Gambling is her only vice. Anyway, I know she can stop if she wants." Or "Stop making such a big deal about his marijuana use. I smoked when I was that age and, besides, it's legal in this state." Denial eventually becomes family members' own primary compulsive activity.

Meanwhile, as the disease of addiction worsens, the addict develops two core beliefs: (1) *I am not an addict*, and (2) *I can control my behavior*. These form the addict's view of him- or herself and the heart of his or her identity. Often the addict's family also adopts and echoes these beliefs about the addict and then uses denial to cling to those beliefs. Typically, as addiction worsens, so does denial.

One of the most common manifestations of denial is silence. In some of my other writings, I describe the "Don't Talk" rule, which people in addictive families typically follow. Family members stop talking honestly about what is happening in the family, and eventually a conspiracy of silence develops. As one young child said to me, "In our family, we just pretend things are different than how they really are."

This conspiracy of silence is insidious and deeply harmful. Some family members may simply not understand what is really happening, so they don't know what to say. Others may have tried being honest and earnest, but were punished or ignored for it, so they didn't try it again. Or maybe when they did speak up, things actually got worse—with someone yelling, threatening them or another family member, or becoming violent.

Sometimes family members don't speak up because no one else does, and they simply follow everyone else's lead. Or they buy into the belief that addiction isn't what it seems or isn't a big deal or, at least, isn't to be talked about.

One of the biggest causes of a family conspiracy of silence is a sense of loyalty. If Dad, the family leader and breadwinner, is snorting coke in the basement most evenings, family members may feel they're betraying him and accusing him of being a bad person by talking about his cocaine habit. While Samantha is getting straight As in school and excelling in gymnastics but also steadily starving herself, her parents keep silent and fear intervening in her anorexia would hurt her chances of getting college scholarships.

In the short term, denial is often an effective defense. That's why so many people use it. It helps them to temporarily avoid pain and, sometimes, to avoid reality. In the long run, of course, it only encourages problems to grow, but it can help people get through a difficult day, hour, or moment. When you have no hope of changing a painful or undesirable reality, denial often feels like an easy, useful, rational choice. It temporarily kills the pain and at the same time creates blind spots in your perception and awareness.

When Denial Fails

As addiction worsens, there eventually comes a time when family members can no longer live in denial. By this time, the family is usually being torn apart. Its members begin to admit to themselves and each other that the addict has a problem and something needs to be done. At this point, the family typically shifts into a preoccupation with the addict and his or her illness. This can take many forms:

- Trying to limit or control the addict
- Lecturing the addict and/or trying to talk sense into him or her
- Accommodating all of the addict's dysfunctional behavior
- Taking on the addict's responsibilities, (e.g., doing her chores or returning phone calls and emails for him)
- Quietly cleaning up the messes the addict leaves behind
- Trying to block the addict's access to his or her addictive activity or substance
- Threatening to leave the addict and/or have him or her arrested
- Punishing the addict by refusing to talk to or be around him or her

- Blaming someone—the addict, the addict's friends, the culture, or a family member—for addiction
- Worrying obsessively about what the addict will do next
- Cancelling family plans in the hope of limiting or avoiding the damage the addict may do
- Mentally reliving some of the terrible things the addict did in the past
- Imagining detailed scenarios of what terrible things the addict might do in the future

Whatever form this preoccupation takes, it begins to control family members' thoughts, behavior, and lives in much the same way addiction controls the thoughts, life, and behavior of the addict. This aspect of the disease is called **codependence**.

By this time, most healthy boundaries among family members have been erased. Previously healthy interactions have been replaced with people talking over each other, avoiding each other, blaming each other, or failing to protect or respect each other. It's also at this point when the addict typically develops an increased tolerance for his or her addictive substance or behavior. In a parallel fashion, family members experience an increased tolerance for the addict's inappropriate behavior.

Myrna used to feel horrified when her drunken boyfriend called her horrible names. Now she just shrugs it off. When Kyle's teenage daughter insists that she hasn't been drinking, even when he can smell alcohol on her breath and see the neck of the Jack Daniels bottle in her purse, he no longer thinks twice about it because he expected it.

As the addict spirals downward, so does the family.

Eventually, the addict loses all control over his or her own behavior. Meanwhile, family members lose all control over their own responses to the addict's behavior.

Here is how the partner of an alcoholic described this stage of the disease: "I was upset; I strongly suspected what he was doing. I planned to not react in rage, as I had in the past, but as it got later and later and he still wasn't home, I began to imagine where he was and what he was doing; so I gathered up all his clothes and set them on fire in the backyard."

At this point, the illness of addiction controls the entire family, whose members all find themselves caught in addictive behaviors. Meanwhile, the family as a whole, as well as each of its members, has become increasingly emotionally isolated. Eventually, everyone in the family is living a life of secrets.

Here is perhaps the most important thing we now know about addiction: it is not just one person's disease. It impacts everyone it touches, and in families it can be as infectious as the flu.

A young boy once said to me, "Addiction is like dominoes. It knocks down the person who then knocks down everyone, including himself."

CHAPTER THREE

Addiction, Trauma, and the Family

When most of us wake up in the morning, we can reasonably assume that our home, our family, our job or school, and our primary relationships will still be there when we go to bed that night. We can also expect the way someone treats us that morning will be more or less how he or she treats us that evening. Our world is generally stable, and we expect it to stay that way. And, most of the time, it does.

This is not true in an addicted family, where nothing is ever stable or predictable. Everything is confusing and unknown; anything can happen at any time.

Darby, who is in active addiction and uses alcohol and meth, may smother her daughter with affection one moment, threaten to punch her a minute later, and then, two minutes after that, tell her she plans to take her out shopping.

In an addicted family, no one knows who is responsible for what because the normal boundaries have been shattered. No one has any idea how to make anything better. And everyone is constantly anxious, frightened, worried, and confused. You never know when something small—a dirty plate in the sink, a bad haircut, a thermostat set a degree too high—might turn into a catastrophe. As a result, family members become apprehensive about the smallest decisions. Meanwhile, outrageous and hurtful things and major, deeply important life decisions may go ignored and unaddressed. There is no more perfect recipe than this for creating trauma.

A Steady Diet of Trauma

When a family is ill with the disease of addiction, its members are much more likely to experience trauma than non-addicted families. That trauma is also likely to be more serious and more painful, and it is likely to take longer to heal. In short, addiction worsens every dimension of trauma.

Addiction creates chronic losses for everyone in the family system: a loss of trust, connection, intimacy, stability, honesty, fun, clear communication, safety, and healthy boundaries. And that's just in the earlier stages of addiction—as the disease progresses, family members also lose jobs, relationships, financial stability, health, and sanity. Children often lose their childhoods by being forced to take on adult family roles. Sometimes people lose their lives.

As one loss gets compounded upon another, the result is usually trauma. In addition to the many losses, chronic emotional abuse is especially prevalent in addictive family systems. It can take any or all of these forms:

- Verbal abuse (ridicule, name calling, etc.)
- Severe criticism and blaming
- Lack of expressed love, care, and concern
- Unrealistic expectations
- Shaming and humiliation
- Broken promises
- Lying
- Unpredictability
- Sudden rages or ravings
- Overly harsh (or outright cruel) punishment
- Being forced into physically dangerous situations (such as being in a vehicle with an impaired driver)
- Breakup or abandonment of the family

In an addicted family, it's hard to find an emotional middle ground. People vacillate from one extreme to the other, often over-responding, often withdrawing, or running away. People have trouble staying in the present and in their bodies. They either live mostly in their heads—reliving the painful past or imagining a horrible future—or entirely in their emotions, consumed with fear, anger, or dread.

There is much for everyone in an addicted family to be legitimately angry about: broken promises; an awareness that the addict cares more about getting and using whatever his or her drug or activity of choice is than about family members; repeatedly being discounted, lied to, abused, ignored, or asked to do the impossible; and having to listen to other family members make excuses for the addict. Over time, this chronic anger can create a trauma response of its own.

The same is true of deep, chronic embarrassment. Who wouldn't be embarrassed when Mom suddenly launches into a loud, drunken tirade in a restaurant? Or when Dad makes a pass at his fourteen-year-old daughter's best friend? Or when your sister shows up at a family member's funeral wearing a tank top and shorts, smelling like she hasn't showered for a week?

There is also a great deal for members of an addicted family to feel sad about. Sadness is a healthy response to occasional disappointment, difficulty, or bad news. But in addicted families, all of these tend to be chronic. When an addicted parent repeatedly fails to show up for soccer games, parent-teacher conferences, music recitals, and class plays, that parent's child's repeated sadness can eventually morph into trauma. The same is true if Dad or Mom does show up, but is sometimes drunk, high, or disruptive.

In addicted families, trauma can also result from guilt. Sometimes this guilt is both legitimate and appropriate, but in addictive family systems, it is often **false guilt**, i.e., guilt for something that isn't actually their fault or responsibility. For children, false guilt tends to continue long after they grow up and leave the family.

Here is how two of my clients described their own guilt:

Mylie: "I felt guilty for causing Mom's depression. She said it was my fault because I didn't always behave just the way she wanted."

Kent: "I felt guilty for the rages Daddy would fly into when I
              didn't guess what he was thinking or anticipate his needs.
              He told me I was the cause of his cocaine use. He said that
              everything in his and Mom's life was fine until I was born."

In some addicted families, members may feel guilty for something as
serious as a parent's death. When James first came to therapy at age forty-
three, he was actively suicidal and struggling with severe depression. I soon
discovered he was consumed with constant, extreme guilt. As we explored
that emotion, he told me about a night when he was twelve years old.
His father came home very drunk, as usual, and started to yell at James's
mother for not doing everything the way he'd told her to. As he bullied and
accused her, she did her best to calm him down and appease him. None of
this worked. James's father got angrier, louder, and more physical.

Tired of witnessing his father's regular abuse and his mother's equally
regular passivity, James grabbed the keys from his father's coat pocket. He
threw the keys at his father and screamed, "Dad, why don't you just go kill
yourself?"

James's dad screamed at James and his mother for another few minutes.
Then he took the keys, stormed out of the house, got in the car, and
headed down the road at high speed. He was killed in an accident twelve
minutes later.

Over thirty years after the accident, James still believed he had caused
his drunken father's death. For three decades, he had been tormented by
guilt—and the resulting trauma—for a tragedy that was not his fault.

Genuine guilt is the uncomfortable, and appropriate, feeling that
results from harming someone or something, committing an offense, or
violating one's own standards, morals, or values. With authentic guilt
people have the opportunity to accept responsibility for something they're
genuinely responsible for.

But in many addictive family systems, people literally don't know
what they're responsible for and what they aren't. Personal boundaries may
be vague, or may shift suddenly and capriciously, or may not exist at all.
Family members may also routinely blame each other for things that aren't
actually their responsibility.

James's guilt over the death of his father was false guilt. Emotionally, he had taken responsibility for his father's actions. For James, though, this incessant, profound guilt, which was never his to carry, led to severe depression and suicidal thoughts.

The most important question to ask yourself is "What am I actually responsible for here?"

Trauma and Abandonment

Abandonment comes in two forms: physical and emotional. When abandonment is chronic, both forms can be equally traumatic.

We've all heard the familiar stories of physical abandonment: the infant left in a cardboard box in an alley; the young child left alone at home while her parents are at the casino; the elderly and isolated parent ignored for several days while her adult son disappears on a drinking binge; also the blatant acts of physical abuse and sexual abuse, when one's body is not respected but used as an object.

Emotional abandonment is much more common than physical abandonment, and it comes in a wide variety of forms. It can be intentional; or the unintentional result of immaturity, inexperience, or cluelessness; or a direct side effect of addiction. For example, Mom can't drive Tessa to her dance class because she's passed out on the floor.

Emotional abandonment typically becomes traumatic when it is chronic. Whether it's personal or situational, or whether it's premeditated or accidental, usually doesn't matter. It is repeated abandonment that tends to evoke a trauma response.

In addictive family systems, emotional abandonment most often occurs between a parent and his or her offspring. It is the job of parents to be available to their children. Parents need to monitor them, care for them, encourage and support them, and express their love for them. Parents also need to keep their children from getting into serious trouble.

No parent does this perfectly and none should be expected to. But when parents chronically ignore or reject their parental responsibilities, they emotionally abandon their child. And when a child is repeatedly abandoned, emotionally or otherwise, he or she almost always suffers trauma.

There are many ways people experience emotional abandonment. The first is simple neglect. This is when a parent is indifferent to a child's needs and wants or is routinely emotionally unavailable or chronically fails to provide support, encouragement, nurturing, affection, protection, and/or supervision. The Adverse Childhood Experience Studies (US Department of Health and Human Services (USDHHS) Administration for Children and Families, 2008) revealed that in homes where there is substance abuse, children are 4.2 times likelier to experience neglect than kids from homes without addiction. The National Center on Addiction and Substance Abuse at Columbia University estimates that substance abuse is a factor in at least 70 percent of reported cases of child maltreatment.

In addicted families, neglect frequently takes the form of inadequate supervision, such as leaving very young children in the care of their slightly older brother or sister all day or forcing kids to wait for hours in a car while Dad is in a bar, a casino, a strip club, or at his dealer's house.

In addicted families, the neglect is often physical as well. Kids aren't always fed or clothed properly. They may not get taken to the doctor when they're sick. They may be sent out to play in the street or to ride their bicycles without wearing helmets. Or a parent may fail to intervene and provide protection when a child is being physically or sexually abused.

In an addicted family, the neglect often goes still further: the roles of parent and child are reversed, with the parent expecting the child—no matter how young—to take care of him or her and meet his or her needs. Thus the child becomes deprived of his or her childhood.

Another form of emotional abandonment involves requiring a child to hide his or her needs, feelings, and/or parts of who he or she is in order to be accepted, approved of, and perhaps even taken care of.

This puts the child in an inherently trauma-inducing situation, because he or she feels forced to learn to follow these impossible-to-follow rules:

- It's not okay to make a mistake. You must do everything right, all the time. Do this even when you have no idea what right is; when no one knows what right is; or when right is whatever the parent decides it is at that moment. And when you do make a mistake or do anything less than perfectly, it's because there is something wrong with you.
- Never fail at anything, even tasks that are impossible or that you're trying for the first time.

- Live up to every family member's expectations, even when those expectations are unrealistic, contradictory, absurd, unstated, and/or completely unreachable.
- Never reveal any vulnerability, uncertainty, or ambivalence because if you do, someone will hurt you or take advantage of you.
- Never show your feelings. If you do, you may be told that what you feel is wrong ("Stop blubbering like a spoiled baby; it's only a broken toe") or ("I saw what happened; that didn't really hurt you").
- Never express your needs. The message is that your needs are not important or that the needs of someone else in the family are more important than yours. If you do express a need it's ignored or dismissed.

Emotional abandonment also involves not allowing a child to have his or her own accomplishments or successes. If the child does, the addict neither respects nor acknowledges those accomplishments.

Although this type of emotional abandonment is less common than the first two, it is just as likely to evoke trauma responses. Here are some variations on this theme:

- A construction worker angrily says to his son, "What do you mean you want to go to medical school? You think you're better than your dad?"
- An entrepreneur berates her daughter: "You're still spending all your time and energy in competitive swimming. How many times have I told you that's never going to earn you a dime?"
- A harried single mom says to her teenage son, "So you got good grades. What do you want me to do, sing and dance? What I need you to do is get an after-school job and contribute to this family."

Abandonment is also when they see their child as an extension of themselves, and demand that the child pursue the parents' goals or fulfill the parents' dreams. Or they may tie their own sense of self-worth to what the child says, does, and looks like. This usually happens when parents have a distorted or undefined sense of personal boundaries. It can also occur when a parent expects the child to take responsibility for the parent's feelings, thoughts, and actions. "If you kids would just behave better, I wouldn't be so stressed and upset and yell at you all the time."

Abandonment also takes the form of the adult not recognizing the child as a child and instead treating the child like an adult. "We're going to the casino. Be a good girl and make dinner for yourself and the twins."

More often than not, parents will emotionally abandon their child in two or more of these ways at once. Whatever the form, abandonment always hurts. Repeated abandonment is traumatic. Sometimes it's so severe, as one of my clients eloquently put it, "While I know I experienced abandonment, I often feel I was never claimed in the first place."

The Trauma of Physical and Sexual Abuse

Departments of child welfare consistently report that in homes where there is substance abuse, children are significantly more likely to be physically and/ or sexually abused. In research conducted by myself, Steven Bucky, PhD, and Sandra Padilla, PhD, we found that in alcoholic families fathers were ten times more likely, mothers four times more likely, and siblings twice as likely to be physically abusive to a child than in families without substance abuse issues. The study also indicated daughters are twice as likely to be sexually abused than in other families; sons are four times as likely to be sexually abused— both by family members and by people outside of the immediate family. My clinical experience suggests that there is often more than one abuser over time.

We don't have good statistics on physical and sexual abuse in homes where there is a process addiction, but my forty-plus years of working with addicted families suggests that the numbers are similar.

Here is what we know about abuse in addictive family systems:

- The ultimate act of physical abuse is murder; however, far more common abuse involves being hit, slapped, shoved, kicked, pinched, or slammed against a wall.

- In addicted families, discipline or punishment can often turn into abuse. This typically takes the form of extreme and inappropriate punishment. For example, forcing a child to stand on one foot for ten minutes, and then beating him when he falls over. In other cases, addiction can turn a somewhat less harsh punishment into abuse, such as when a child is sent outside to stand on a cold porch for a few minutes to "think things over," and then left there all night because her parents have passed out. Often a punishment isn't particularly severe, but it is inflicted capriciously on a child who has done nothing wrong.

- Sexual abuse is both overt and covert. Overt sexual abuse involves sexual touch. Covert sexual abuse of a child involves no touch, but can take many other forms, such as shaming him or her about his or her body or sexuality; sexual name calling (such as calling the child a whore or a slut); graphic sexualized joking; exposing the child to pornography; or using sexual innuendo. For example, Dad tells his thirteen-year-old daughter, "You are so hot-looking. I wish I were your age, so I could have a shot at you."

- The more frequent the abuse, the more likely the victim is to minimize and rationalize it. As sixteen-year-old Kailie told me, "No, I wasn't abused. My mom didn't mean to break my jaw when she hit me."

- When a child has two addicted parents, the likelihood of physical or sexual abuse is substantially greater than when only one parent is an addict.

- In addicted families, abuse is especially hurtful on days of celebration, such as holidays, birthdays, anniversaries, and graduations. Often the celebration itself gets undermined, revoked, or denigrated. One client told me, "I cannot count the number of Christmases I would get up in the morning in anticipation of opening the presents, only to find they had disappeared over the course of the night. Somehow I knew that it was connected to the fact that I had done something wrong the day before."

- In cases where the addicted person perpetrates the abuse, the abuse may or may not occur only when he or she is drunk, high, or otherwise engaged in an addictive activity. In fact, some addicts abuse kids or partners only when they are abstinent. This is particularly unnerving and disturbing for the victimized family members, as it looks to the victims as if the abuser is making a deliberate, conscious, well-considered choice to harm them.
- When physical and/or sexual abuse occurs in an addictive family system, people usually assume the addict is the abuser. But this is not necessarily the case. Surprisingly often, a parent or sibling who does not suffer with addiction is the abuser.

Abuse can spread throughout a family in much the same way addiction does. Remember, addiction is a disease that infects the entire family, not just the addict.

My professional experience has also taught me that when a parent is abusive to one or more of his or her kids, at least one sibling is likely to be physically or sexually abusive toward at least one family member as well. Often an older abused child becomes the abuser of younger children in the family.

In other cases, one child is singled out as the sole or primary target. The targeted child is often the one whom an abuser unconsciously perceives as being most like him- or herself. The abuser then becomes determined to punish and/or control that child. Sometimes the targeted child reminds the abuser most of his or her partner and thus stirs the abuser's misplaced hostility. Sometimes the abuser targets the most passive child, because that child is the one most likely to accept being victimized. And sometimes an abuser targets a strong-willed or defiant child, abusing the child in an attempt to make him or her subservient.

Certain attributes make a child more vulnerable to being abused:

- The child is starved for love or attention, and a perpetrator outside the home grooms him or her for abuse under the guise of friendship.

- The child is unlikely to speak to others about any abuse because the family system is infested with lies and denial; either the child simply will not be believed, or the child believes he or she will not be believed. Or, because of the family's dynamics, and/or the child's prior victimization, the child feels powerless. Someone who feels powerless is not likely to tell another person if he or she is victimized, especially since the child has no hope that anyone will help or care.
- Because of widespread dysfunction in the family, the child doubts his or her own experiences and perceptions.
- The child is already so traumatized that he doesn't know what he feels, and can't rely on his own emotions or intuition as cues and signals to let others know he needs help.
- Because family members have poor personal boundaries, the child is already confused about what boundaries are appropriate, what is normal, or who is responsible for what.
- The family is suffused with shame, which discourages its members from speaking up, making waves, or telling the truth.

Carolina, a victim of physical abuse who was raised in an addicted family, described what regularly took place in her home.

> I can remember being a little girl, and I had drawn on the wallpaper in our breakfast room. I thought it would look prettier if I used my best crayons. My mom was so upset for the rest of the day that I had no food, no bathroom break, and no escape. I was sent to my room and was told to wait for my father's punishment, which meant being whipped with his thick leather belt. I actually don't remember the beating, but I do remember the anguish of waiting all day for the dreaded event. As I waited, one of the things that I would do was bargain with God, praying that maybe my daddy would hit me only once and it would be with his hand. Or maybe, if he had to hit me, it would not be so hard. My wishes never came true. The drunker he was, the more he was out of control.

At a very young age, Carolina learned how to bargain. But because the abuse was chronic and unavoidable, she also knew that she was powerless in her bargaining. She knew in advance there would be no fairness, no flexibility, and nothing to negotiate with her father. That's why she tried to bargain with God or fate.

Later, when she grew up and left the household, she knew she would have to find strength in her resilience to advocate for herself or succumb to being a perennial victim.

Witnessing Abuse

Watching a person go through traumatic events—for example, watching someone leap from the window of a burning building—can be traumatic. Furthermore, trauma is usually more severe when the event being observed involves abuse. It is more severe still when both the abuser and the victim are members of your own family—and when you are helpless to do anything about it.

This phenomenon, sometimes called the **witness factor**, was first formally recognized in the 1840s. Over the years, in military contexts, it has also gone by the names **Soldier's Heart** and **shell shock**. These days it is considered a form of **post-traumatic stress disorder**, or PTSD.

The witness factor plays a much bigger role in trauma than most people realize. During the Vietnam War, the American military began to recognize a counterintuitive reality: if two soldiers have equal combat exposure, and one becomes physically injured, the one who is not injured is more likely to experience PTSD. The witness to any horrific event may experience more trauma than someone who was physically harmed in that event.

For example, a child who witnesses the repeated abuse of a family member, but is not abused himself, may experience strong bouts of survivor guilt, usually mixed with great sadness, fear, helplessness, and rage.

In some cases the child may also imagine that because she has been spared the abuse, she has the ability to defuse the situation or protect other family members. Usually, though, when the child attempts to use this imagined power, she fails. Sometimes the child may also become a target of abuse.

Here is how some witnesses of abuse in addicted families described their experiences:

Craig: "My two sisters, just a few years older than me, didn't do as well in school, so they got beatings for poor grades when report card time came around. It was horrifying to see Dad hit them so hard that blood came out of the welts on their legs. I felt so guilty and so ashamed for not being able to protect them."

Steven: "When I was about ten, Dad would regularly come home drunk about three in the morning and drag my brother out of bed. He would beat Larry with his fists to make my brother a man. Then Dad would hold him up to the mirror and say, 'Is this what a man looks like?' The tears and look of fear that filled my brother's eyes were also my tears and fears. I always wondered when Dad would try to make me a man."

It should come as no surprise that addicted families tend to experience higher-than-average rates of murder, suicide, premature death, accidental death, house fires, car accidents, gun accidents, other forms of serious injury, and serious illness. For the survivors in the family, all of these create trauma.

Overlooked and Discounted Trauma

In addicted family systems, people don't just act in ways that tend to evoke trauma responses. They also tend to respond with less love, caring, and support whenever a traumatic event occurs. In a moment of crisis, family members may be unable to solve problems, perceive options, seek resources, or even pay attention. This can be particularly damaging for children.

A gang of boys approached fifteen-year-old Darlene one day as she walked home from school. They grabbed her and tried to drag her into the woods, but she managed to break free and run home. Gasping and in tears, she told her mother what had happened. Her mom just lifted her martini and said, "Well, honey, you learned something important about boys today, didn't you? Now leave me alone for a while. I'm watching my favorite TV show." In the space of a few minutes, Darlene was traumatized twice—first by the boys, then by her mother.

Seven-year-old Jonathan was walking to school with his friend Heather on an icy winter day. Suddenly a slow-moving car skidded off the road and struck Heather, and she fell in a heap by the roadside. People gathered around her and did what they could to save her life, but she died an hour later in the emergency room. Throughout the event, everyone ignored Jonathan. This was partly understandable, because there was a dying girl a few feet away. But Jonathan's experience of watching his friend die was traumatic for him nevertheless.

Jonathan's trauma never got addressed. Everyone—his classmates, his teachers, his principal, his parents, and even the driver of the car, who was also traumatized by the event—focused on Heather and her family. When Jonathan tried to tell his parents how terrified he felt, they told him, "Do you realize how lucky you are? That could have been you who died. Count your blessings that you got to school without a scratch." Then they lit up a joint.

It took Jonathan two more decades before he finally got treated for depression. Only then did he have a chance, for the first time, to talk about "little Jon," who had watched his friend Heather die.

Doya grew up in a home filled with rage and substance abuse. But things were better at school, where she was popular and had lots of friends. Then the family moved from Denver to a small town in Georgia. At her new school, Doya was the only Native American, and she was chronically made fun of and bullied. Her parents, who were preoccupied with drinking, doing meth, and earning a living, acknowledged the bullying, but not her pain. "This is what white people do," they told her. "Remember your uncles Jack and Jerome? White people put both of them in jail. You have to get tough."

Kevin was born with cerebral palsy. He was a bright and inquisitive child who was normal from the waist up, but needed many surgeries on his legs. As a result, he was in and out of hospitals until he was in eighth grade. While his mother was often with him in the hospital, what he remembers most was her incessant crying—not about him, but about his father, who was an alcoholic and a compulsive gambler.

Today, Kevin recalls the hospital nurses and orderlies fondly. But he doesn't remember his father ever coming to the hospital. Nor does he remember his mother touching him much or doing anything to comfort him. He recently told his therapist, "I don't know whether Mom came to the hospital to be with me or to escape Dad. I felt safe in the hospital—not because of Mom, but because of the nurses, and because Dad wasn't there."

Painful and difficult things occur in every child's life. Parents can't protect their children from every painful event, but they can respond in a manner that lessens the negative impact. Unfortunately, in addicted families, children are often denied caring and empathy at vulnerable times. As a result, traumatic events usually affect them with full force.

How Trauma Encourages Addiction

So far, we've looked at how addiction encourages, spreads, and deepens trauma. But the opposite is also true: trauma can make the brain more vulnerable to addiction in much the same way a poor diet can make the body more vulnerable to infection.

It's common for people with unhealed emotional trauma to turn to addictive substances or compulsive activities in an effort to medicate or numb their pain. This closely parallels the experience of people recovering from physical trauma, and who are vulnerable to becoming addicted to painkillers.

The Adverse Childhood Experiences Study (ACE), a landmark study emanating from the mid-1990s and continuing to be replicated today through the Centers for Disease Control and Prevention in Atlanta, clearly states that the greater the number of adverse childhood experiences, the more it contributes to:

- Early initiation of alcohol use
- Higher risk of alcohol abuse
- Prescription drug use and illicit drug use
- Drug dependency and self-reported addiction

It's important to remember, though, that vulnerability—a reduced ability to ward off illness—is different from inevitability. If you walk around outdoors without a jacket in forty-degree weather, you're more vulnerable to cold viruses than someone who keeps warm, but you might not come down with a single sniffle. That said, if you've got unhealed trauma, monitor yourself carefully. Be alert for warning signs of addiction.

The Trauma/Addiction Cycle

As mentioned previously, addiction often encourages trauma, and trauma can encourage addiction. This process can become what is often called a vicious circle or a negative feedback loop, with trauma contributing to addiction, which in turn fuels more trauma, which encourages still more addiction, and so on.

Here are some examples of how this process plays out in people's (and families') lives:

Brent

Brent grows up with a father who is highly critical. Nothing Brent does ever seems good enough for his father. He routinely compares Brent to his two older brothers, who are both excellent athletes and consistently get high grades (TRAUMA).

In contrast, Brent struggles in school, and Brent's father repeatedly accuses him of being stupid and lazy (TRAUMA). (Later, in his twenties, Brent discovers he has a learning disability.) Brent's mom—a professional singer who is on the road most of the time—is distant, busy, and preoccupied (TRAUMA). She leaves most of the child-rearing to her husband.

In high school, Brent becomes part of a group of close friends who spend much of their time partying together. Together, they find solace in drinking and smoking weed (USING DRUGS TO SELF-MEDICATE). Brent especially likes that they don't have to please their parents or, at least, don't try to. By the time Brent is twenty-five, he is addicted to alcohol and pills (ADDICTION).

One night, as he drives home from a party with his buddy Gary, his car hits a patch of ice and spins out. Brent does his best to regain control of the car, but he has had four beers and his reaction time is slow. The car tumbles into a deep culvert. Gary breaks both legs (TRAUMA); Brent suffers a serious brain injury (TRAUMA). He is put on pain pills, which only further fuels his out-of-control drug use (ADDICTION).

Jenna

At age fourteen, Jenna is raped by three assailants (TRAUMA). Her parents report the crime to the police, but Jenna is terrified, ashamed, and in shock, and refuses to talk about it with anyone.

Soon after that, her attendance at school becomes sporadic. At age fifteen, she begins periodically cutting her arms with razor blades. By age sixteen she is using pills, and by age eighteen, meth (ADDICTION). By the time Jenna is twenty, most of her friends are fellow addicts. On her twenty-first birthday, her boyfriend sells her for sex to their dealer in exchange for drugs (TRAUMA).

Kim

Kim grows up with a severely alcoholic father and a hypercritical mother (TRAUMA). From the time Kim is in kindergarten, her mother is preoccupied with Kim's size and weight.

Soon after Kim turns nine, her dad goes into rehab and stops drinking. A month after that, her mom reveals that she has had a longtime boyfriend and runs off with him (THE TRAUMA OF ABANDONMENT).

For the next eight months, Kim's parents fight over her in an angry and acrimonious divorce (TRAUMA).

At age fourteen, Kim finds herself exercising excessively to keep herself thin. About once a month, she binges on tons of junk food, then sticks her finger down her throat and vomits it up (BULIMIA NERVOSA).

She also begins to party hard—drinking excessively and taking large amounts of opiates. One night, when she is drunk, she passes out and is raped by several of the guys at the party (TRAUMA). One of them posts a brief video of the rape on social media (TRAUMA).

Kim's humiliation, shame, and inability to reach out to her parents continue. So do her partying, bulimia, and drug use. And so do the sexual assaults (TRAUMA).

By age twenty-four, Kim uses heroin and alcohol addictively (ADDICTION). By age thirty-one, she has tried to kill herself three times.

Julie, Leo, and Bryce

In late 1998, Julie fell off the horse she was riding (TRAUMA). Her pelvis was seriously injured, and her doctor prescribed oxycodone during her recovery. Her recovery was slow but complete. Unfortunately, in the process she became addicted to pain pills (ADDICTION).

Three years later, Julie's husband Raul, a firefighter, was one of the first responders to the 9/11 attacks. He was in one of the towers when they collapsed; his body was never found in the rubble (TRAUMA).

Suddenly widowed, with traumatized children ages seven and nine, Julie began to drink herself to sleep each night (ADDICTION). At first the kids didn't seem to notice; they were in their own state of shock, and neither one knew what normal was anymore.

As the months and years passed, Julie's drinking and pill usage kept her in bed longer and longer (ADDICTION). She became moody and unpredictable. The kids became more self-sufficient, asking less and less of her. This enabled Julie to take even more pills and alcohol (ADDICTION).

By the time Leo, the oldest child, turned fifteen, Julie would regularly swing from one mood to another. Sometimes she was profoundly depressed, sometimes nearly manic, occasionally overly reactive, and at times disengaged from everything. She provided little structure and support for the kids other than meals, clothing, and an occasional hug (THE TRAUMA OF ABANDONMENT).

In response, Leo threw himself into school and school-related activities. His younger brother Bryce stayed in his room compulsively surfing the internet and playing video games, becoming steadily more isolated from the world.

Eventually, through an intervention led by her physician, Julie was able to stop using and get into recovery. She woke up to an older son in community college who was quite responsible, and a younger son who was showing signs of gaming and porn addiction (ADDICTION).

The Bottom Line

Here are the four most important things I hope you'll remember from this chapter:

1. Disaster, physical harm, and sexual abuse are not the only sources of trauma; they are simply the most visible and obvious ones.

2. Physical and sexual abuse is considerably more common in addicted families than among families in general. Nevertheless, in addictive family systems, the less obvious and visible sources of trauma—especially chronic abandonment—are far more common still.

3. Trauma and addiction routinely cause, encourage, and reinforce each other. As a therapist, whenever I see one, I've learned to always look for the other.

4. It is possible to recover from both trauma and addiction, even when they are both quite serious. Because they so often interact, they need to be treated together—not as two separate, unrelated conditions.

It's important to stay grounded when you are reading about that which can be extremely personal. There can be so much to absorb. This is a good point in your reading to pause, breathe, and engage in an act of self-care.

CHAPTER FOUR

How Trauma Affects You

An essential part of healing from your trauma is recognizing the ways in which trauma has affected you. In whatever ways you have responded to the trauma in your life up to now, these responses are not:

- Preset, lifelong patterns from which there is no escape
- Flaws or sins for others to use to judge you or for you to judge yourself
- Signs that you are inherently weak or damaged; or
- Indications that you are going crazy

They are simply signals that you have been hurt.

Your trauma can be healed with care, attention, time, patience, proper treatment, and sound recovery practices. In fact, you have already begun your healing process by reading this book.

The Inner World of Trauma

Please read the following descriptions of trauma responses with empathy and openness. As you read each one, regularly check in with your own heart, body, and mind. If you recognize yourself in any of these responses, write down in your journal or notebook how you experience that response or how it gets acted out in your life. These notes will be enormously helpful in your own healing, especially as you read later chapters and in any therapy you may choose to undertake.

The primary emotion that accompanies trauma—both at the time of the traumatic event and later, whenever the trauma gets triggered—is strong and overwhelming fear. However, a great many other responses are possible as well. Let's first take a close look at the different **short-term responses** to trauma. These tend to appear immediately or soon after the traumatic event; the affected person may experience one, several, or all of them.

If a traumatic event occurs only once—for example, if someone loses their home in a flood—then the body's natural healing mechanisms may adequately address the trauma over time. As a result, these responses may slowly wane and then disappear once a sense of safety has returned. However, when trauma is repeated and chronic—for example, during civil wars or in addicted families (which often become miniature civil wars)— the trauma is not likely to heal on its own, and these short-term responses are likely to persist.

> **Hypervigilance:** People who recently experienced trauma may feel that danger is always lurking. They are constantly on guard, scanning their environment for threats and wary and distrustful of everyone and everything. This is the body's way of always being prepared for more trauma.
>
> **Hyper-reactivity:** After a traumatic event, people are often over-sensitized to small potential (or imagined) threats, responding to them with intense fear, anxiety, anger, or panic. They may have exaggerated, startled reactions to loud noises, quick movements, and other sudden or unexpected experiences. When their trauma is triggered, they may instantly have an over-the-top fight, flee, or freeze response—often without even understanding what is making them so upset.
>
> **An inability to focus:** Someone who is so focused on scanning the surrounding environment and anticipating danger may have little mental bandwidth left for anything else. This can impair the ability to think, concentrate, or learn. It can also be overwhelming and exhausting. As a result, the person may become forgetful or spacey.

Extreme emotional reactions: Emotional reactions to trauma can vary greatly. After the traumatic event has passed, the ones most likely to surface are anger, fear, sadness, and shame. People may suddenly, without warning or a clear cause, find themselves immobilized in terror or crying incessantly or become extremely agitated or suddenly and unexpectedly lashing out in anger. They may experience deep feelings of inadequacy. They may swing quickly from one extreme emotion to another. Understandably, they feel overwhelmed by their own emotions and/or unable to control them.

Dissociation: When one's trauma is overwhelming, yet it is impossible to physically remove oneself from the situation, an individual may emotionally and mentally leave his body. The individual feels completely disconnected from the world, or as if floating above it. This is an extreme form of the flight response and a survival mechanism for getting through a time of great (or perceived) danger and terror. When dissociation occurs during a traumatic event, it can actually help preserve someone's sanity.

Trauma expert and author of *The Body Keeps the Score*, Bessel van der Kolk, MD, says, "Dissociation is adaptive: it allows relatively normal functioning for the duration of the traumatic event and then leaves a large part of the personality unaffected by the trauma."

Dissociation can also cause those affected by trauma to lose chunks of time from their memory, as if they had been unconscious, even though during that time they were clearly awake and interacting with others. Dissociation isn't just a human experience. It occurs routinely in the animal world. If you were to watch a video of a pack of wolves attacking a deer, you'd see the deer's eyes glaze over just before it stops struggling. An automatic dissociative response has kicked in, separating its mind from its body and protecting it from extreme pain.

Here is how one young man described his recurring experience of dissociation in the midst of abuse:

I would stay home alone with my mother on the weekends while my father was on his binges. She'd drink one drink after another and begin talking about how men and women were different. Then she would begin her striptease and tell me to touch her. After that she would lead me to the bedroom, where molestation would take place. I was so confused; I was so scared. If my father knew what the two of us were doing, I was sure he would kill me—and probably Mom, too.

I still remember the first time. It was as if my whole nervous system was on fire. Right in the middle of what we were doing, I started to cut out. There was this splitting, this separation, and I was no longer in my body. At that moment, finally I felt safe. It was as if I went to a new dimension. I stayed there until the sex was over and I could go back to my room. Then I came out of the fog.

Dissociation is understandable. When you cannot physically run away, and when you cannot stand and fight, you emotionally and mentally flee your body.

Flashbacks and other intrusive memories, thoughts, and feelings: Traumatic events can get stuck in the body and our reptilian brain. These parts of us have no sense of time, only an awareness of now. As a result, many people who suffer from trauma find themselves mentally and emotionally reliving their traumatic events over and over. This reliving sometimes involves a **flashback**, in which the person re-experiences—via sight, sound, smell, touch, taste, or some combination—portions of the traumatic event.

Reliving such an event in flashbacks can sometimes be worse than the original event itself, because flashbacks can occur repeatedly, often without any warning, at any time—even during sleep. Many people who suffer from flashbacks organize their lives trying to avoid them or protect themselves against them. This constant battle with internal dangers can become exhausting. Meanwhile, real-life events can seem less compelling in comparison, and it can become harder to feel the joy of ordinary life or concentrate on the tasks at hand.

Flashbacks are usually triggered by something that reminds the person of the event behind his trauma. But sometimes these experiences occur randomly and without warning or are triggered by something too small for the person to consciously notice.

Disturbed sleep and/or nightmares: Not surprisingly, most of the above trauma responses can interfere with sleep. It's hard to fall asleep, stay asleep, and awake refreshed when your mind is going a mile a minute or when you feel you need to be hypervigilant to remain safe. Once you do fall asleep, you may find yourself reliving the traumatic event, either literally or symbolically, in nightmares.

A desire for alcohol, other drugs, and/or compulsive behavior: People who are in great emotional pain much of the time look for ways to numb themselves to it. Some do it through alcohol, marijuana, pain pills, cocaine, heroin, or other drugs. Others numb themselves through over-indulgence or compulsive relationships with food, sex, work, social media, gambling, porn, shopping, people, or anything with a screen (a computer, an Xbox, a smartphone, etc.). There is some genuine internal logic to this: when something hurts and you don't know how to heal it, you find a way to blunt the pain.

Denial: Some people respond to trauma by denying—to others and/or to themselves—that they have any feelings associated with their traumatic experience. This is another way to attempt to blunt the pain. Often denial and a desire for an addictive substance or behavior go together.

Delayed Responses to Trauma

Many trauma responses are delayed, emerging weeks or months after a traumatic event. Often they appear so much later that the person experiencing them doesn't connect them to the trauma. Unfortunately, sometimes health and mental health professionals don't make the connection either. A skilled and conscientious mental health professional who observes one or more of these responses in a client will ask the client about any potentially traumatic events in his or her past.

The most common **delayed trauma responses** are:

Rigidity and avoidance: Trauma can sometimes create a long-term, wide-ranging freeze response in which a person is unable to handle any new or unfamiliar situation. Anything strange, unpredictable, or unscripted may unleash an interior wave of terror; as a result, the person avoids anything he or she can't control or predict—which, of course, is most situations and people.

Some people who have experienced trauma avoid intimacy and close relationships in general. These relationships feel terribly dangerous, partly because they are by nature unpredictable, partly because they make people more vulnerable.

Fear of dying or having a shortened life: Trauma often affects someone's beliefs about the future. The person may experience a loss of hope, limited expectations about life, and/or a fear that his or her life will end abruptly or early. "I doubt that I'll live to be over thirty," a twenty-five-year-old woman once told me. She was physically healthy but she had been sexually abused as a child, and raped at age nineteen.

In other cases, people with trauma simply can't imagine they will ever live normal lives. Getting an education, having a positive and committed romantic relationship, or getting a good job and building a career all feel like fantasies to them.

Numbness: People with trauma sometimes feel that having any emotion—even a pleasurable one—is dangerous. Over time, they learn to equate a loss of control with a loss of their sanity, so when they do experience an emotion, they feel like they're losing their mind.

In response, they cut themselves off from their own emotions, their own body sensations, or both. Eventually, they may have little or no emotional response to anything. They become emotionally numb.

Another route to numbness is the "Don't Feel" rule, which is common in addictive family systems. In such families, people learn that it's not safe to experience (or at least show) their emotions. Or else they learn their emotions—their fear, sadness, anger, anxiety, and dread—are useless in helping them avoid danger or abuse. And in some families, life is so painful and dangerous that people have little joy and little trust that anyone will attend to their needs and emotions. In all of these cases, people flee their own emotions and go numb.

Learned helplessness or chronic victimization: One way to describe trauma is the experience of being helpless and choiceless while being harmed. Some people who have suffered trauma, especially severe or repeated trauma, later generalize from that experience—sometimes weeks, months, or even years after the event. This can result in:

- A sense that they have no choice about anything in their life
- A belief that they are helpless in any and all situations
- A belief that they were, are, and always will be a victim
- A feeling that there's no point in planning for the future

These convictions can quickly become self-fulfilling prophecies. The traumatized person diminishes his or her life by refusing to make decisions, take risks, pursue goals, make choices, or clearly state his or her preferences or desires. Meanwhile, potential abusers quickly spot these individuals as potential victims, zero in on them, and lay their traps.

People who see themselves as victims usually have trouble saying no or setting limits and boundaries. They may even feel they have no right to do so.

Victims typically develop a high tolerance for pain and for others' harmful or inappropriate behavior. They become highly skilled at rationalizing, minimizing, and often flatly denying the painful events and emotions in their lives. They frequently fear that if they did call out others on their hurtful behavior, this would only invite more trouble.

When someone feels helpless to stop or blunt repeated trauma, this person believes she may not suffer as much if she gives in, doesn't fight the inevitable, and subordinates herself to someone else. Unfortunately, that "someone else" almost always increases the abuse being inflicted.

Self-injury: One counterintuitive but not uncommon response to trauma is a desire to injure oneself.

Most people who have an urge to harm themselves follow through with it only once or twice. For other trauma sufferers, however, it can become a long-term compulsion.

This impulse makes no sense to the thinking brain; why try to escape from persistent pain by creating more pain? But there's a bodily logic to it. The act of harming oneself often generates a dissociative response or a feeling of release and relief. It is also a way to try to regulate painful emotions such as anger, anxiety, sadness, and shame. Here is how one person with trauma described her own compulsion to cut herself:

> People always want to know what it feels like, so I'll tell you: there's a sting when you first slice, and then your heart speeds up when you see the blood because you know you've done something you shouldn't have, and yet you've gotten away with it. Then you sort of go into a trance, because it's truly dazzling—that bright red line like a highway route on a map that you want to follow to see where it leads. And the sweet release, that's the best way I can describe it, kind of like a balloon that's tied to a little kid's hand, which somehow breaks free and floats into the sky. For just this moment I am free from the pain of my life.

Of the trauma responses that involve self-injury, cutting and burning are the most common. But self-injury can take many other, less visible forms, such as the incessant pinching of skin, or even something as extreme as swallowing bits of ground glass. People who feel a compulsion to harm themselves are often very creative at hiding this behavior from others.

Compartmentalization and secrecy: All of us compartmentalize at times. While we're focused on a topic or task, we temporarily set aside our feelings and thoughts about everything else. This brings order to our day and allows us to be fully present and productive.

Compartmentalization enables you to have a conflict with your partner over breakfast, but then mentally set aside the conflict during your workday when you need to focus on your job. It also enables you to mentally and emotionally return to the conflict once you leave your workplace so you can arrive home and say, "Hey, I've got an idea about how to solve our dilemma."

But extreme or compulsive compartmentalization can be a trauma response. Imagine you're twelve years old, and every night you fall asleep to your parents shouting at each other and calling each other names. You'll soon learn to mentally and emotionally set aside the previous night's argument when you go to school in the morning. And when your coked-out father points a gun at you one afternoon, then laughs and says, "Just kidding," you may set aside your fears and worries in order to be able to eat supper and do your homework. By compartmentalizing your painful experiences, you say to the world, "I've found a way to be okay in spite of the madness in my household."

However, over time, what begins as a necessary defense might evolve into a habitual form of denial. Eventually you may end up living a double life, presenting a public face of stability and happiness, but privately feeling miserable and lonely. Ultimately, this ability to compartmentalize can encourage great secretiveness, which in turn strongly enables addiction. I see this with many of my clients. To the outside world, their lives seem fine, perhaps even exemplary. But in private, they are compulsive gamblers, or gamers, or porn users. Meanwhile, no one around them has a clue, because they are so good at compartmentalizing each aspect of their life.

Daniel: "I was very skilled at living in two worlds, or even three—home, work, and my outside world of sex. They were different compartments of my life that were never to meet. I was masterful at lying and simply couldn't allow myself to think about my work, colleagues, or wife finding out about my secret life. Since I was a kid I've been living in different worlds; I lived with terror at home, so I'd escape into my sexual fantasies and then find relief at school. So the compartmentalizing came easy."

Patty: "Each morning as I left home and went into the day, it was as if I crossed an invisible line. I didn't think twice about how what I was doing would affect my family life. I truly didn't think about it."

An attraction to dangerous or high-risk situations: Some people with trauma are drawn to dangerous or high-risk situations that replicate their past trauma. In seeking these situations, they may be unconsciously trying to relive and correct the experience or safely complete the action they weren't able to complete before. This enables them to establish a kind of retroactive control over the traumatic incident, at least symbolically.

If someone's trauma was chronic, this attraction might have a different purpose. The person's internal compass has become oriented toward the excitement, the sense of rush connected with surviving danger. If a person routinely feels numb, these situations may be the only ones in which they feel alive or connected to their body. Most of us take it for granted that safety feels good. But if you were raised in a home where safety was not the norm, you might lack this reference point.

Distorted and/or extreme anger: Anger is a normal response to exploitation, betrayal, violence, or an event that seems threatening or unfair. It also helps us focus our attention, thoughts, and actions on survival and gives us increased energy for persisting in the face of obstacles. Anger is also a way for us to claim power in a situation that might otherwise render us powerless. All of these attributes make anger a central—and quite appropriate—feature of many trauma responses.

But some people who experience trauma get stuck in their anger, which can later get triggered by ordinary events and situations. They may respond to these everyday occurrences with sudden rage, as if their lives were being threatened. But rage is more than anger. Rage is the accumulation of one's humiliation, shame, and fear. The wrathful person is disengaged from all of the feelings beneath their anger. They may become furious when someone gives them an odd look or passes them on the highway or tells them, "I'm sorry, but we're all out of chicken rice soup." Some of these folks walk through life with a metaphorical gas can in one hand and a lit match in the other—and almost anything can ignite their rage.

Post-traumatic distorted anger typically has three interactive aspects:

1. *Heightened arousal.* Any hypervigilance or hyper-reactivity that appeared soon after the traumatic event has become habitual. The person regularly feels tense, irritable, keyed up, or hyper-alert. He or she is constantly on the lookout for danger, which naturally makes him or her easily provoked. This is especially common in people whose trauma was chronic.

2. *Uncontrolled or habitual behavior.* The person may have difficulty modulating or controlling his or her anger. The person may also respond habitually to any threat— whether real, potential, or imagined—by aggressively protecting him- or herself.

3. *Unrealistic thoughts and beliefs.* We all have core thoughts and beliefs that help us understand the world and make sense of it. But people with post-traumatic distorted anger

typically sense—or believe—that threats are everywhere. Their core thoughts and beliefs make the world seem more dangerous and less predictable than it actually is.

Each of these three aspects tends to reinforce the other two, creating a vicious cycle of pain, uncontrolled aggression, and disruption. Let's look at a couple of examples:

Samuel is a former combat soldier who knows in his bones that following rules and carrying out orders were what kept him alive through multiple battles. Now he is safely back home, but he has not yet healed his trauma. He suddenly flies into a rage when his small children are playing with their food at dinner.

Krystal was raised by a demanding and controlling mother who insisted that she follow every household rule to the letter and spanked her for the smallest infractions. When Krystal's husband Bill gets home ten minutes later than he promised, she suddenly goes ballistic on him, calling him every derogatory word in the book.

Neither Samuel nor Krystal understands the source of their distorted anger. In fact, while each of them rages, a voice inside their head asks, *Why am I going so crazy over this?* Beneath their rage is unhealed trauma.

Chronic physical pain: When physical trauma severely damages the body, it usually creates acute physical pain. But emotional trauma can also create a great deal of physical pain. This pain frequently becomes chronic.

Trauma embeds strong emotions—terror, sadness, grief, shame, and/or fury—in the body. If the trauma remains unhealed, over time these emotions can create a variety of physical symptoms, such as back and neck pain, headaches, or sore muscles. These symptoms can often be severe, making it difficult to function; sometimes they can even be disabling.

There are numerous studies that link chronic pain with those who have experienced various forms of childhood trauma. My colleague Mel Pohl, MD, a pioneer in the treatment of chronic pain and addiction, tells me that almost every one of his clients who has chronic pain also has a history of unhealed trauma. There are several theories as to why this is so, with some evidence pointing to the chronically heightened stress response (due to trauma) in the same parts of the brain that register pain.

Physical illness: When trauma has not been healed, the trauma responses—especially delayed and prolonged ones—can eventually create physical illnesses. The most common ones are digestive and autoimmune problems. The highly regarded Adverse Childhood Experience Study I referred to in Chapter Three reveals a strong relationship between childhood trauma and physical health problems, including diabetes, heart disease, and cancer. When our bodies are pushed past their normal limits, especially repeatedly, they begin to break down. Our long-term trauma responses can tax our bodies and create inflammation, compromising our immune system, which in turn makes our bodies more vulnerable to illness.

Chronic health worries: One long-term response among some trauma sufferers is an abnormally heightened concern about their health. This may appear instead of or in addition to actual health issues. Symptoms include:

- Frequently or compulsively worrying about real or potential illness
- Interpreting normal physical sensations or ordinary symptoms of minor illness, such as a slightly sore throat, as signs of serious physical problems
- A fear that ordinary physical activity—working out, gardening, etc.—may damage the person's body
- Repeatedly checking their body for abnormalities
- Seeing healthcare professionals frequently and feeling these visits don't relieve their concerns, or that these visits actually worsen their concerns
- A general sense of fear around the health and safety of their body

Major depression and dysthymia: The word **depression** has multiple meanings, so let's begin by sorting these out. Most people will tell you they have felt depressed at times. What they usually mean is that they have felt a mixture of sadness and helplessness for a longer period than felt comfortable or normal to them. This is not clinical depression, but what some therapists call **low mood.** (Low mood is an informal, shorthand description, not a diagnosis.) Experiencing a low mood now and then is actually quite normal.

Furthermore, when sadness and helplessness correspond to a recent trauma or loss, this is a completely normal and appropriate response. If you have always paid your taxes fully and honestly, and you get an unexpected letter from the IRS saying that you owe $30,000 from five years ago, it would be odd if you *didn't* feel some despair and futility. You might find yourself agitated and want to isolate yourself from everyone for a while.

But this low mood wouldn't persist indefinitely. After a few hours—or, at most, a few days—you'd begin to lick your wounds and strategize about what to do next.

Like low mood, **grief** also superficially resembles clinical depression in some ways. If you're grieving, it's normal to feel sad; you process these feelings and move through them, and eventually they subside. It might take you weeks, months, or even years to complete the process, but you are not stuck. Over time, you do heal. (It is true, however, that people who don't adequately grieve a loss can have that grief turn into depression over time.)

Major depression is a fundamentally different experience from low mood or grief. Someone with major depression can only see and feel the bad side of everything. Every experience is ultimately disappointing. Many people with depression routinely (or constantly) feel a deep, profound sadness; others live with an emotional numbness that makes them unable to feel anything at all.

Major depression often has a strong genetic influence. But it can also be largely psychological, stemming from one or more of the following forms of trauma: repeated psychological injury and chronic stress; being raised by one or more parents with a habitually pessimistic view of the world; extreme (or repeated) unprocessed sorrow and grief; repeated experiences of significant defeat. In many people who have experienced trauma, depression has both psychological and biological origins.

A much less severe (and more common) form of depression is called **dysthymia**. People with dysthymia feel an absence of joy in their life or routinely feel stuck or stifled. Often they have low energy. Still, they are able to function most of the time. In many people, dysthymia comes and goes, either in cycles or at random; in some, however, it can settle in and become a way of living.

The symptoms of major depression are usually quite obvious. However, many people with unhealed trauma struggle with dysthymia, sometimes for years, yet have no idea they have it or even know what it is. They simply accept its symptoms as their normal mood. Someone with dysthymia may have a good life and may even know that it's a good life, but he or she simply can't feel a lot of joy or contentment. Something always seems to be amiss or missing or not quite there.

Whether or not someone is experiencing major depression or dysthymia, what is so apparent is the role of self-loathing. Self-loathing creates a vicious circular pattern, in that being depressed causes self-loathing and the self-loathing (shame) fuels the depression.

Untreated, any form of depression can last months, years, or even decades. But remember: if you have depression and a history of trauma, your depression is almost certainly a symptom of the unhealed trauma. Medication alone will not adequately address it.

As previously noted, not only can depression be a delayed response to trauma, but when combined with compartmentalization the two responses merge into what I call **closeted depression**. While I believe this description is extremely validating to many people, it is not a clinical diagnosis.

Here is how closeted depression manifests: some people have the ability to compartmentalize and are able to hide their depression from most or all of the world, sometimes for months or years. Yet untreated depression—and unhealed trauma—tends to worsen over time. When someone lives with closeted depression for months or years, his or her internalized hurt, disappointment, fear, and anger fester and build on each other. To handle this, the person may disconnect from his own feelings or his own body. Meanwhile, the individual systematically avoids sharing who he is or what he feels with anyone. He may also cover up his depression by staying busy, accomplishing many tasks, and appearing extremely competent. By deliberately focusing people's attention on other things and other people, the individual surrounds himself with an impenetrable force field that says, "Don't ask me about myself, and don't push me."

Eventually this structure collapses. Usually that collapse is triggered by a loss of some kind. Sometimes, though, the burden of hiding and compartmentalizing everything simply becomes too heavy, and the person's protective mechanisms stop working. Then the depression takes over, in a way that is clearly visible to everyone. Paradoxically, this is a huge step toward healing. Other people are now in a better position to help and support the person, so he can address his trauma.

My client Caleb described his experience with closeted depression—and his eventual meltdown—this way:

> I had always lived like this. I functioned. I operated in the world. I had a good job—most people would say a great job. My family appeared quite happy. I have great social skills in facilitating other people's joy and comfort. But the minute I am not busy, not focused on other things, I am left with my own self-loathing, critical self. At times I have even thought about suicide. No one, not even my closest friends, knew how I felt over the years.
>
> Then, one day, I just couldn't keep up the pretenses. None of my old defenses were working. It was there, like the silent intruder who was hidden in the closet all of these years.

High anxiety: Most people feel a little anxious while solving a problem, taking a test, or making an important decision. This is actually a good thing: being slightly anxious tends to improve people's performance. But being excessively anxious has the opposite effect.

An anxiety disorder is a serious impairment. Someone with the most common anxiety-related condition, called **generalized anxiety disorder**, experiences unrealistic and excessive worry, tension, and anxiety for little or no cause. It's as if the person's brain and body are caught in a loop of self-perpetuating anxiety. People with this disorder typically want constant reassurance from others, yet even when they get it, they don't feel any better.

Generalized anxiety disorder causes so much distress that it interferes with the person's ability to lead a normal life. Often it disturbs his or her family, friends, neighbors, and coworkers as well, as they attempt (usually unsuccessfully) to manage or work around that person's anxiety.

Generalized anxiety disorder sometimes occurs in tandem with depression. The person with both conditions shifts back and forth between having little energy and enthusiasm in one moment and then feeling great anxiety and agitation in the next.

A second type of anxiety impairment is **panic disorder**. This involves sudden surges of overwhelming anxiety and fear—what is often called a panic attack. This is intensely physical, not just emotional. In a panic attack, the person's heart starts beating rapidly and he or she shakes or sweats heavily.

The first panic attack often occurs at times of stress, but the triggers can be enormously broad. In some cases triggers may be unidentifiable to the person in that moment. They are most often related to feelings that seem unmanageable. It's as if a short circuit in the brain suddenly pushed a neurological panic button.

In the midst of a panic attack, the physiological symptoms can be so severe that you may think you're dying. You may even end up in an emergency room clutching your chest, only to be told that physically you're fine.

Phobias: A **phobia** is a lasting and irrational fear involving a particular object, person, creature, or situation. People can (and do) have phobias of literally hundreds of things—from heights to enclosed spaces, to the sight of blood, to the feel of meat. In severe cases, a phobia can be brought on by a memory, image, thought, or mere mention of whatever the person fears—for example, a drawing of a spider or a photo taken from the top of a skyscraper.

Being scared of angry or aggressive dogs is not a phobia; it's an appropriate protective response. But if you're scared of all dogs—or all German shepherds, including ones that are friendly or sleeping—that's a phobia.

One particular type of phobia is a condition called **social phobia** or **social anxiety**. This is a cross between generalized anxiety disorder and a phobia. Someone with this condition is excessively worried and self-conscious about everyday social situations. The worry often centers on a fear of being judged by others or of behaving in a way that might cause embarrassment or lead to ridicule. As a result, this person often limits her social encounters, and/or uses alcohol and other drugs to lessen her fears and fortify her courage to be able to engage with others.

Obsessive control of others: Controlling or manipulating others is a way to try to create some physical and/or psychological safety. It's a learned behavior that in an addictive family system is often a form of survival. It's learned so innocently, such as being the child who makes sure your siblings are at the dinner table before Mom and Dad get there because it's more likely to lessen Dad's anger; or making sure the car gets put into the garage after your father has passed out at the wheel in the front yard so that the neighbors don't see it and think poorly of your dad or the family. You find ways to create a greater sense of safety to compensate for the overwhelming experience of fear and powerlessness. It's such a strong defense and in the moment brings greater safety and order to a fearful and chaotic situation that it becomes a finely honed skill that people readily take into adulthood. Unfortunately, it often becomes a primary way of relating to the world and can cause difficulty in most all areas of life.

As one of my clients told me, "When I manipulate people, places, and things, I feel most powerful. It may be a false sense of power, but I will take a false sense of power any day over no sense of power." Another explained, "I've got to tell you, it felt a lot better to bully the other girls than to be the victim one more time. It was bully or be bullied, and I certainly had enough of that at home."

The greater the chaos and trauma in someone's life, the more desperately that person may feel the need to control everyone and everything. Any uncertainty or any relinquishing of control feels deeply risky. Compromise, negotiation, vulnerability, and openness all seem terrifying rather than safe and empowering.

But if that's how you get by, day after day, over time this survival mechanism can become your habitual way of dealing with others and the only way you know how to relate to other people. This diminishes your life, as well as the lives of most people you encounter.

Tragically, skill in manipulating and controlling others is sometimes rewarded in the workplace and even praised as a leadership quality.

Perfectionism: Unfortunately, in a family affected by addiction a child learns "No matter what he does, it's never good enough." As a result, in the child's struggle to feel good about himself and relieve the source of pain, he constantly pushes to excel and to be the best. The result is these children often do things quite well, yet never feel good about themselves or what they have done, always believing they could have done it better—"It's not good enough" becomes translated into "I am not good enough."

The child's entire sense of safety can be dependent on the approval of others. Yet this approval is often capricious, based on someone's mood or state of sobriety, or how his or her day has gone so far.

Children are often expected to be excessively mature for their age. Eight-year-olds are expected to cook dinner for the family. Six-year-olds are expected to change diapers. Yet these same children are also taught there is no room for mistakes and that if they make even the smallest infraction, something bad is going to happen. This is a tried-and-true recipe for trauma. It also tends to create perfectionism. Perfectionism is driven by the belief that if one's behavior is perfect there will be no reason to be criticized and therefore no more cause for pain. The perfectionist does not just operate at 100 percent; he or she operates at 150 percent. Anything less sends him or her into a spiral of self-defeat and thoughts of being inadequate or a failure.

Long after a perfectionist has grown up and left the confines of her family, she may continue to feel that if only she would do everything just *right*, she will avoid pain.

This feeling may also get generalized and projected onto others: the person feels that if only everyone else were to do everything right, the world would be a much better and much less painful place. Consequently, controlling others with perfectionistic beliefs creates a barrier between the perfectionist and those he or she cares about, be it friends, siblings, or partners.

Perfectionism is a serious threat to the mental health of people, fueling depression, anxiety and, at times, suicidal ideation.

How Disorders Pair Up—or Pile Up

As discussed, people's long-term trauma responses can be simple or complex, mild or severe. Imagine one day, while you're at work, someone bursts in with a gun and begins shooting at random. You and most of your coworkers get out safely, but two people—both of whom you know—are killed.

You'll probably be traumatized by that event. Most people would be. But, depending on a dozen different factors, you might come out of the experience with only one of the conditions described in this chapter. Or, at first, you might experience only one of them; but over time, others might emerge. Eventually, if you leave your trauma untreated, a variety of painful symptoms can accumulate and reinforce each other, creating a tight knot of issues and difficulties.

One well-known form of this accumulation is PTSD, which stands for **post-traumatic stress disorder**. PTSD is described as a set of accumulated, chronic, unprocessed fight, flight, and/or freeze responses. (You might also have heard the term *post-traumatic stress symptoms*, which describes the more common and less severe short-term trauma responses described near the beginning of this chapter.)

Post-traumatic stress disorder is as much about *post* (which means after) as it is about trauma. One of the features of PTSD is that symptoms don't usually appear until long after the traumatic event—usually three months to several years later. As a result, when symptoms do first appear, they may seem to come out of nowhere; however, the underlying trauma was there all along. It just took some time for the symptoms to manifest.

Some people recover from PTSD on their own within six months or so, while others have symptoms that last much longer for years or even decades. In some people, the condition can become chronic.

These symptoms generally include a combination of the many responses already presented: intrusive memories; avoidance; negative changes in thinking, mood, or body cycles; and/or changes in emotional reactions, such as persistent overreactions, startle responses, or chronic emotional numbness.

People with PTSD are also extremely likely to have some form of depression, as well as anxiety and a behavioral and/or substance addiction.

What makes PTSD so serious, and so potentially damaging, is that for someone with the condition, the traumatic event comes to dominate how he or she organizes his or her life. The person perceives most of the stressful events in his or her life in the light of his or her earlier trauma. Let's look at two examples.

Twenty-year-old Allison is currently in a treatment program for heroin addiction. Growing up, she was sexually abused by her brother for eight years. She later found solace in opiates, beginning with prescription pain pills and eventually moving on to heroin. When I first met her, I immediately noticed the many scars on the back of her legs and arms, signs that she had repeatedly cut and burned herself, probably for years. In addition, as I sat with her in group therapy for the first time, it appeared to me that she had the hiccups. After several minutes, and later confirmed by the clinical staff, I realized she was not having hiccups but in fact was having startle responses. She was reacting to noises outside of the group room, such as the sounds of a door slamming, another person talking, or a car horn honking. Her head would suddenly jerk, then the jerking subsided almost as quickly as it started. Allison was struggling with the ability to feel safe and clearly suffering from PTSD.

Sam grew up in Manhattan with his parents and brother. On September 11, 2001, while home alone, he watched on television as the Twin Towers came tumbling down. Sam was sixteen at the time.

Sam's father died in the attack. His mother escaped unharmed, but she was unable to call to tell him that she was alive. She stayed behind to assist survivors, so she did not make it home until late that day. Sam spent the day glued to the television, watching the horror unfold, and concluded that both his parents had died. Although he was thrilled when his mother finally returned home, over the next few years he repeatedly experienced sudden, unpredictable flashbacks of the towers crumbling and people jumping to their deaths.

Thirteen years later, Sam is married and has a four-year-old son, Frank. The last of his flashbacks occurred several years ago. Then, as Frank and Sam are crossing a street a taxi hits Frank, and for several days Sam and his wife do not know if he will live. Frank does survive, but he is hospitalized for several months.

Two months after Frank's injury, Sam begins suffering from sudden, debilitating panic attacks, each one followed by week-long episodes of feeling nothing but doom and despair. He sleeps less and less, lying awake and staring at the ceiling for hours.

Eventually, Frank fully recovers; however, by the time he is released from the hospital, Sam has developed a habit of drinking half a bottle of gin each night in order to fall asleep. He routinely shows up late for work, and his marriage is starting to fall apart.

Sam clearly suffers from PTSD and is in early stage addiction.

Making the Turn

This chapter has painted a detailed picture of the effects of trauma. That's deliberate. I want you to begin to recognize the signs and symptoms of unhealed trauma, both in yourself and in others. Now for the good news: there's a tried-and-true way to effectively deal with every one of these trauma responses. That healing is the focus of the chapters to come. First, though, let's take a closer look at an emotion that frequently looms large in addicted families and that can also be an outcome of trauma: shame.

CHAPTER FIVE

Shame: The Hidden Darkness

Shame: the painful feeling associated with the belief that who you are is not good enough, that you are inadequate, you are not worthy, and you are not of value. People often confuse guilt and shame. Yet there is a profound and fundamental difference between the two. **Guilt** is synonymous with remorse. It is what you feel when you realize you have *made* a mistake that could cause harm. **Shame** is the sense that you *are* the mistake. When you experience shame, you feel there is something inherently wrong with who you are as opposed to what you have done.

Shame makes you feel alienated, defeated, and never quite good enough to belong—to your family, to your community, to the human race, or to the world. And since you don't (and can't) belong, you feel disconnected from everyone. There is also a sense of being exposed and vulnerable, of needing to hide your flawed or inadequate parts from yourself and others.

I strongly concur with Brené Brown in her book *Daring Greatly*; it reads:

> We all have shame. We all have good and bad, dark and light, inside of us. But if we don't come to terms with our shame, our struggles, we start believing that there's something wrong with us—that we're bad, flawed, not

good enough—and even worse, we start acting on those beliefs.

Many trauma responses are in fact manifestations of shame. Your perfectionism, rage, and controlling behavior are attempts to garner power over your shame. Addiction is a way of medicating the shame. Depression and victimization are often ways you succumb to the shame. In short, shame is a deep internal darkness, a psychological and emotional prison. Worse, it's a prison you believe you deserve to be in, because you're so inherently flawed or worthless. This is why, in his book *Shame: The Power of Caring*, therapist Gershen Kaufman describes shame as "without parallel, a sickness of the soul."

How Shame Arises

No one is born with shame. Like racism or xenophobia, it is something we learn, usually from an early age. Our culture implants shame in us. It gives us messages that we don't belong—or aren't good enough—unless we look or dress or act or speak a certain way; unless we're a certain weight and body type; or unless we're familiar with whatever TV programs, celebrities, sports teams, and social media are currently popular. Experiencing a small amount of shame is common, everyday shame is normal and unavoidable. Experiencing chronic or ongoing shame is not.

Most of us first learned shame from our families when we were young; however, in a healthy family not much shame gets taught or passed on. Conversely, in an addicted family, shame doesn't just get sprayed on people now and then. It gets poured on family members, day after day, until they're drowning in it. And, in general, the less functional a family is, the more shame it spews on its members.

As previously noted, where there is addiction, there is often unhealed trauma. Shame is one of the most common and pernicious responses to trauma—especially repetitive, unavoidable childhood trauma. Consequently, where there is addiction, there is often unhealed shame. Shame, addiction, and trauma routinely go hand in hand.

You may recall from Chapter One that developmental trauma is trauma inflicted repeatedly on someone by a person he or she knows and can't avoid. Usually this involves a parent or someone in a caretaking role traumatizing a child. In the initial stages of experiencing trauma, that person's natural internal response is, *Why is this happening to me? What did I do wrong to deserve it?* But when similar traumatic events occur over and over, this internal message changes to: *Why is this happening to me? Could I deserve it because I'm bad or unworthy?* Eventually the message morphs further into: *This is happening to me because I deserve it, because I'm inherently flawed, unlovable, and undeserving.*

This is how shame becomes internalized, and then regenerated over and over through trauma. Unhealed, this shame tends to continue long after the traumatic events have ceased. Living or growing up in an addicted family typically means experiencing such developmental trauma, often for years. Its members rarely realize that what is happening to them is not their fault—especially since a parent or other powerful adult may tell them it is their fault. Meanwhile, the addictive family system may be so chaotic, and personal boundaries so distorted, that no one in it can offer protection from what is happening.

How Shame Masks Itself

If you become angry with someone, you'll probably know it immediately. You'll feel the anger, recognize what it is, and choose what to do about it. The same thing happens when you are bored or hungry or excited or frightened. But shame isn't like most emotions. People rarely think, *Hmm, I'm feeling shameful now,* or *Hey, I'm in my shame!* Instead, they'll think thoughts like these:

> *Man, I'm such an idiot.*
> *I can never do anything right.*
> *There I go again, saying something stupid. Look at me. What a screwup.*
> *I failed again! No surprise there.*

And those are just the thoughts they're consciously aware of. Beneath these conscious messages are subliminal ones like these:

> *I'm not important.*

I don't deserve to be happy.
I'm a big phony.
I don't belong.
I'm nothing.
I'm defective.
I am damaged.
I am broken.

One of the hallmarks of shame is this ongoing self-deprecating inner dialogue, which rarely gets outwardly expressed. Some clinicians and researchers describe shame as a feeling, but my experience as a therapist has taught me that shame causes people to actually disconnect from their feelings and become numb to them. Shame is not so much an emotion as it is an emotional block. The greater someone's shame, the more numb he or she tends to become.

When someone begins the all-important work of healing his or her trauma, inherent in the process will be the healing of shame.

This is another good point in your reading to pause, breathe, and engage in an act of self-care.

CHAPTER SIX

Generational Reverberations: The Long-Term Effects

Trauma begets trauma and addiction begets addiction and each tends to beget the other. Both can reverberate throughout a family system and get passed down to the next generation and then the next. If left unaddressed, they may continue to be felt in many lives, over many decades. This chapter looks closely at these generational reverberations.

Neither addiction nor trauma responses tend to spontaneously erupt in anyone's life. But that's how things can sometimes appear. Addiction may skip a generation, much like certain genetic traits. Although it was there all along, embedded in the family system, it was temporarily hidden—only to reappear a generation later.

A Mother in Trouble

Let me introduce Therese, who ultimately became one of my clients.

Depression   Anxiety

Therese's first interaction with the mental health system is when she is shuffled into a community clinic on the arm of a neighbor. The therapist who first sees her quickly recognizes she's suffering serious depression. Her speech is slurred; she is unable to make any decisions, even small ones; she does not care for herself well (she is sloppily dressed and poorly groomed); and she has exceptionally low expectations for herself and her life. Because her depression is so severe, at first the therapist wonders why Therese hasn't been hospitalized.

In this first appointment, the therapist learns Therese has been divorced twice. Both of her former husbands were addicts. In both cases, they were the ones who left the marriage. At the conclusion of the session, the therapist and the consulting psychiatrist prescribe antidepressants—quite appropriately, given the severity of Therese's depression. Therese agrees to return in a few weeks.

When she does, her energy and attitude are different. She is consumed with anxiety and exhibits the symptoms of generalized anxiety disorder. She explains to the therapist that during the past few weeks she has been to the emergency room twice, each time thinking she was having a heart attack. In each case, tests confirmed her heart to be healthy, but she was diagnosed with panic attacks. The therapist also learns that Therese frets and worries about every minor detail in her life. Everything is a potential problem for her. Just needing to ask someone in a grocery store where the napkins are sends her into a panic.

The therapist and consulting psychiatrist recognize that Therese has what is known as a **co-occurring disorder**—multiple interacting mental health conditions, both depression and anxiety. They adjust her medications accordingly.

Initially, no one in the mental health system thought of Therese as the ex-wife of addicts, or as someone who grew up in an addicted, trauma-filled household. They viewed her as simply someone seriously ill with depression and anxiety. Looking at her marriages, Therese's second husband was addicted to alcohol, pills, marijuana, and whatever else he could get his hands on. Her first husband was addicted to alcohol. Both marriages were highly conflictual: each husband in his addiction was frequently absent from family life, chronically lied about his whereabouts, and wasn't considerate of any needs of Therese or the kids. As painful as the marriages were, Therese had been devastated when each of these men left her.

Now let's look at Therese's childhood and upbringing. She was raised in an alcoholic family where there was a great deal of emotional abuse and occasional physical abuse as well. While most of her father's abuse was directed toward Therese's mother, he frequently grabbed Therese by the shoulders and either shook or shoved her. He often screamed or ranted at her, with his face close to hers. He belittled and shamed her, and made it clear to everyone in the family that he much preferred her younger brother and older sister. He closely controlled how Therese dressed and wore her hair.

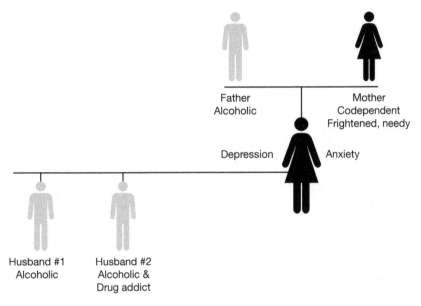

Nearly every night, Therese's parents argued loudly. She would cover her ears with pillows trying to drown out the hurtful things her father was screaming to her mother. Her mother was a frightened, passive woman who went to great lengths to appease and placate her husband, but her efforts rarely succeeded.

Therese's first husband had an alcoholic father and a physically ill mother. Therese's second husband came from a family similar to Therese's, with a rageful, abusive (though not addicted) father and a frightened, needy mother. Together the dynamics of both her husbands' families closely resembled those of Therese's.

Therese had two siblings—a sister who was two years older and a brother one year younger. Her sister died in a car accident when Therese was seven. Her brother was a compulsive overeater as a child; today, as an adult, he is obese and continues to regularly overeat.

Now let's take a look farther up the family tree at Therese's grandparents. Her maternal grandfather was an alcoholic and a compulsive gambler; her maternal grandmother was a compulsive overeater who often flew unexpectedly into fits of rage. Her paternal grandmother died a few weeks after giving birth to Therese's father, leaving him without a mother. Her paternal grandfather lived in chronic poverty throughout his life and was barely able to feed and clothe his son.

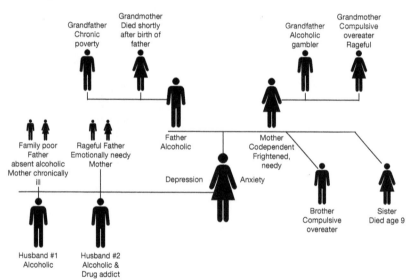

In Chapter One I discussed how certain experiences could help children—and adults, too—become more resilient and less vulnerable to trauma. These are:

- A close relationship with at least one caring, nurturing adult (usually but not necessarily a parent)
- A sense of belonging, both at home and in one or more other places (e.g., school, a neighborhood, a religious group or center,

an organization such as Little League or Girl Scouts, or the home of a grandparent or other relative)
- Activities outside the home that are easy, safe, lawful, and pleasant (e.g., a chess club, school band, or a writing group)
- A sense of success, achievement, or mastery in at least one activity or aspect of life (e.g., cooking, babysitting, skating, basketball, web design, etc.)
- A sense of purpose or meaning in life
- A belief that a positive future lies ahead or at least is possible

Sadly, Therese had none of these as she grew up. Instead, as a child, she learned to:
- Deny, rationalize, minimize, or overlook things others did that hurt her deeply
- Tolerate and make excuses for others' hurtful actions
- Appear cheerful even when she was hurting
- Compulsively avoid conflict in order to minimize or appease others' anger
- Routinely put others' needs ahead of her own
- Take care of others
- Discount her own perceptions
- Give others the benefit of the doubt, no matter how unreasonable or abusive their actions were
- Believe she had no other options
- Believe she was at fault whenever anyone said she was (and sometimes when nobody said anything)
- Not ask others for help
- Not ask questions
- Keep quiet, put her head down (or in the sand), try to soldier on, and hope for the best

Therese's childhood history was a training ground for being part of unhealthy relationships. In fact, she was reared to be the perfect partner for an addict. The form of addiction didn't matter. Therese's codependent traits would support and enable any type of substance or process addiction.

At the time of her initial visits to the therapist at the community health clinic, Therese had sole custody of her two children: a ten-year-old daughter from her first husband and a seven-year-old son from her second husband. The children have already been exposed to their fathers' rages and addictive behavior, as well as their mother's depression and anxiety. All of these traits have carried over from previous generations.

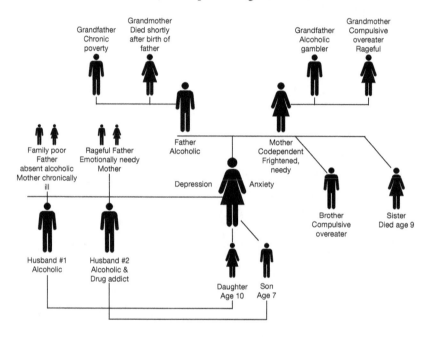

Most therapists agree these seven core experiences encourage kids to grow up reasonably happy and emotionally healthy:

1. Adequate food, shelter, clothing, and safety
2. Healthy role modeling
3. Warmth and support
4. Parental monitoring and supervision
5. Ongoing parental awareness of the child's relationships with friends and peers
6. Strong and healthy parent-child communication
7. Healthy family rituals

During her initial months of therapy and medication, Therese is unable to offer any of these experiences to her kids. Both of her ex-husbands are equally unable (or unwilling). The same is true of Therese's extended family, which has a weak and unstable structure.

By not addressing her own emotional issues, she is also likely to repeat unhealthy romantic relationships. Unfortunately, if Therese's trauma is overlooked and untreated she is unlikely to fully recover from either her anxiety or her depression. She will very likely continue to show up, over and over, in the healthcare system. Therese might seek help in a physician's office, a mental health center, or a family service agency, but she won't get much better. This is because the root of her problems is not being addressed.

The key to Therese's recovery is an acknowledgment of her trauma and deliberate efforts to heal it. Until and unless this occurs, Therese will remain stuck in harmful and repetitive behavior and, invariably, in intense pain. She may have one appointment after another with myriad professionals, but she will stay stuck.

A Son in Trouble

Over the years, as Therese remains stuck in the cyclic loop of trying to heal from her unaddressed trauma, her family continues to follow in her generational dysfunction. Therese's son Rob, now twenty years old, enters an addiction treatment program for young adults. He doesn't want to be there, but he was given two alternatives: treatment or jail time. Rob was busted for selling drugs—his second such offense.

His mother never recognized or attempted to heal any of her traumas. She never remarried, either, though she occasionally had a boyfriend. However, none of her relationships lasted more than a year. Because of on-and-off therapy, plus antidepressants and anti-anxiety medications—both of which she took intermittently—she was able to function well enough to meet her daily living needs. Her episodes of serious depression were few and far between, though she was often too tired to provide much structure or supervision for her son.

In treatment, Rob acknowledged that Therese was a decent mom and let him do pretty much whatever he wanted. In fact, Rob regularly sold drugs online from his upstairs bedroom in his house. He also regularly used them himself. In the days that follow, Rob's counselors learn more details about Therese. Her bedroom is on the first floor and not once in the past three years had she walked upstairs to her son's bedroom.

Therese hadn't asked or expected much of Rob. He didn't finish high school; he just quit going, and his mom never challenged him about it. The behavior and attitude Therese passed down to her son is that of seeing the world through the eyes of being a victim and that life is and will simply always be painful and difficult.

Parenthood in Trouble

The behaviors Therese learned as a child set her up to be a partner in addictive relationships. Those same behaviors (listed on pages 95) also fueled a variety of unhealthy parenting practices. As Rob's mom, Therese engaged in the following:

- Denied, rationalized, minimized, or overlooked her son's irresponsible and sometimes criminal behavior
- Tolerated and made excuses for her son's irresponsible actions
- Appeared cheerful, even when she was confused about why Rob acted the way he did
- Compulsively avoided conflict in order to minimize friction with Rob and avoid his potential anger
- Routinely put Rob's needs ahead of her own; did not respect her own needs; and allowed Rob to take advantage of her
- Did not allow herself to raise her concerns with Rob
- Discounted her perceptions of her son's activities
- Gave Rob the benefit of the doubt even when she had clear evidence that her son was using and selling illegal drugs
- Believed she had no other options and so remained a victim, held hostage by Rob's behavior and choices
- Failed to hold Rob accountable; refused to believe he was at fault
- Did not ask for help. (As she later explained, "I didn't want help; I just wanted him to stop his using and selling.")
- Didn't ask her son about his activities

- Kept quiet, put her head in the sand, tried to soldier on, and hoped for the best

The techniques Therese learned in order to survive her traumatic childhood were the same ones she used to raise her son. It's no surprise she passed on some of her family's troubles to the next generation.

Trauma Bonding

Bonds developed between people can be amazing and wonderful things. Think of the love bond between happily married people or the maternal/paternal bond between parent and child or the bonds between friends. Yet bonds that are every bit as strong but are harmful and toxic can also be formed. **Traumatic bonding** is the result of a continuing cycle of abuse involving intermittent (or alternating) reward and punishment. This creates powerful emotional bonds between the people involved—bonds that are highly resistant to change. Trauma bonding often involves the misuse of fear, excitement, danger, risk-taking, and/or sex to entangle another person. Experiencing extreme situations and extreme feelings together tends to bond people in a special way, which can be both positive and negative.

Trauma bonding typically begins in childhood, with a parent who abuses, physically abandons, and/or emotionally abandons his or her child. When that child becomes an adult, he or she often replicate those trauma bonds with his or her intimate partners and, sometimes, with his or her own children. The only reliable way to break this cycle is to heal the underlying trauma.

Therese grew up in a trauma-bonded relationship with her dad. As an adult, she played out a similar trauma-bonded relationship with her first husband. After he left, she entered into a parallel trauma-bonded relationship with her second husband. As she raised Rob as a single mom, some of the same trauma bonds appeared in their relationship as well. In this way, Therese's trauma bonds with her father spread from generation to generation. Paradoxically, the players' trauma-bonded relationships are often interchangeable. As seen in Therese's life, while the names may change, the underlying dynamics repeat themselves over and over. This is called **trauma repetition**.

Trauma bonding is in part why it is harder to leave an abusive or controlling relationship the longer it continues. And as in Therese's case, she was in two hurtful relationships with addicted husbands and it was they who left her. In fact, after each husband departed, she was emotionally devastated. Sadly, growing up in an unsafe home makes later unsafe situations have more holding power.

New Faces, Old Dynamics

When underlying trauma remains unhealed, a person's trauma bonds tend to replicate in all of his or her intimate relationships—even with people who appear to be nothing like each other.

After a few months of marriage to her first husband, Therese realized he had a problem with alcohol and was drinking addictively. To try to make the marriage work, she ignored his DUIs, cowered when he unpredictably flew into jealous rages, and did her best to be a cheerful, subservient wife. None of her efforts worked. After two years of marriage, he left her for another woman.

Soon afterward, she began dating a man who did not seem anything like her first husband. He was far more educated and articulate, and he made much more money. He didn't drink at all and didn't use illegal drugs. In fact, he often berated people whose out-of-control behavior was fueled by alcohol or other drugs, and he was upset and outraged by how Therese's father had treated her. After a year of dating, they got married.

At first, Therese felt much more taken care of by this husband. But as the months passed, *taken care of* slowly turned into *controlled by*. First he took control of their finances, ostensibly to manage them better. Then he sold her car, telling her they really didn't need to own two. By the end of their first year of marriage, she was largely dependent on him. She had to ask him for money, to use the car, or to do anything outside of their neighborhood.

In their second year of marriage, Therese discovered her husband had used cocaine, alcohol, and prescription pain pills for many years. He became abstinent only a few months before the two met. By year three, he began drinking again. His cocaine and pill use resumed soon afterward. Not long after he started using again, he lost his job and began coming home later and later. Therese also learned he was sleeping around with several other women. Meanwhile, Therese was stuck at home much of the time, alone and isolated.

She tried to make their marriage work, using the same strategies she'd learned as a child and had applied to her first marriage. But, just as they didn't work with her father and her first husband, they failed with her second husband as well. He too left her for another woman or, possibly, more than one other woman. Therese wasn't sure, not that it really mattered. She had learned she couldn't trust anything he said anyway.

Therese's story is quite common. Like most people who formed trauma bonds early in life, she repeatedly reenacted an old, destructive script she learned in childhood. With one abusive person after another, in one abusive relationship after another, she repeats the same painful but familiar experiences, scenarios, and emotions.

Love and Relationship Addiction

As discussed in Chapter One, a form of process addiction is addiction to a person or a romantic relationship. Therapists call this **love addiction**, **relationship addiction**, or **love and relationship addiction**.

Such relationships have all the characteristics of addiction and thus need to be addressed as such. Many people who identify with trauma bonding recognize the addictive nature of their part of the relationship as well.

The foundation of a relationship addiction is the addict's strong and pervasive fear of being abandoned and rejected. Typically, when the addict was a child, his or her emotional needs were rarely or inconsistently fulfilled by his or her parents or, sometimes, by anyone. In such families, a child usually grows up feeling his or her value as a human being can be measured only by his or her relationship to a partner—regardless of how that partner treats him or her.

The signs of a relationship addiction can include:
- The confusion of love with frequent, exciting, and/or high-energy sex
- A history of destructive relationships involving fights, threats of leaving, high stress, and recurrent drama
- Difficulty ending a painful or abusive relationship

- A history of relationships with partners who are unavailable and/or highly controlling
- Intense or even debilitating fear of being without a partner
- Feeling useless and valueless without a partner
- Compromising one's values in order to maintain a relationship
- Not being able to say no
- A lack of clear personal boundaries
- Perceived intimacy that turns out to be fleeting or imaginary
- A concern that one is not good enough for his or her partner
- Unrealistic beliefs or magical thinking about one's partner or his or her relationship with that partner
- Engaging in unprotected or risky sex in order to catch, keep, or mollify a partner, which sometimes results in a sexually transmitted disease and/or an unplanned pregnancy

When a relationship addict is involved with someone, he or she may live in fear that the relationship could end at any time. Yet the addict may also have a new potential partner in mind or waiting in the wings. And when a relationship ends, he or she may hurry to begin a new one, often prematurely or too quickly.

Details vs. Dynamics

One of the things that makes addiction so insidious and enables it to be passed down from generation to generation is that it has multiple stages and a wide variety of manifestations. You can tell yourself, "I will never get involved with anyone remotely like my mother," and deliberately pick a partner who could not be more different from her. Yet, somehow, a year later, you find yourself reenacting your relationship with your mom in exquisite detail—all while asking yourself, "How in the world did I get here?"

Many people who were raised in addicted families don't fully understand the disease. Maybe as kids they didn't experience it in all its stages, so they can be blindsided by a stage that is unfamiliar to them. Or maybe, because they grew up in a family with substance addiction, they have a hard time recognizing some of the more subtle signs of a process addiction. Sadly, many people say, "I knew he was an addict but I loved him despite it; I knew how to handle it." More often than not this speaks to low self-esteem ("I don't deserve more or better"), coupled with a high tolerance for the hurtful and painful. Whatever the reason, people who grew up in addictive family systems frequently marry or partner with addicts, no matter how much they try not to.

You get there in part because there are aspects of addiction you can't yet see or understand, and partly because your own unhealed trauma is causing you to act in certain self-sabotaging ways.

What can finally change this dynamic is not a simple vow to do things differently, but the healing of your underlying trauma.

Exploring Your Family Tree

A family tree is a simplified version of what therapists call a **genogram**. The purpose is to visually depict family background information that sheds light on current issues. It helps you to become aware of familial patterns that are often passed from generation to generation. A genogram reflects the creator's vision of the family at a given point in time. Different family members may have varying perspectives on the family and therefore construct genograms of the same family quite differently. A family tree may also tell you what you don't know about your family and impact you with a deeper level of knowing the reality of your family history.

For most people with a past of addiction and trauma, the visual presentation of what they have drawn or written out in their family tree strongly helps them to recognize on a more visceral level that what they are experiencing in their family is not unique to them. A significant gift in creating a family tree is that it allows you to recognize that you are genuinely a part of a multigenerational system, and that any difficulties you are having did not start with you. You are not the family screwup, you are not the bad egg; in fact, what you are experiencing is systemic. Creating a family tree is not about finding fault or blaming, but to realize that family dynamics fuel a variety of issues. I have often said, when there is active addiction in the family, look again and you will find more of it. And when there is recovery, it will reappear again as well.

Looking back at Therese's story this is what her family tree looked like.

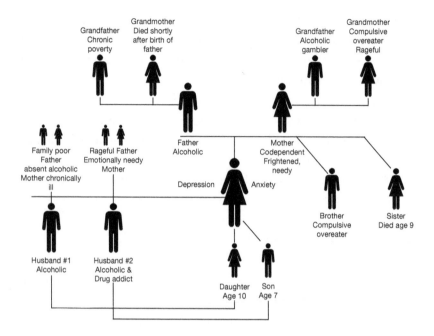

It is apparent that what occurred in Therese's life is not unique to her. For the past three generations there are signs of addiction and trauma and the resulting effects. Her grandparents influenced Therese's parents, and they in turn influenced Therese and her siblings. These multigenerational influences then created reverberations that now influence Therese's children. We also view her husbands' parents, seeing that both were also influenced by similar family dynamics.

Therese's pain-driven responses are depression, anxiety, and repetitious marriages to addicts who are directly connected to trauma bonding and relationship addiction. Her brother's acting-out behavior is his compulsive overeating. A sister who was killed in a car accident added one other dimension of trauma that shaped Therese's life. Without recovery or healing showing up in the family tree, one can see the potential for the influences to continue to impact the next generation—Therese's children.

Here are two other family trees so you can see how dynamics may vary.

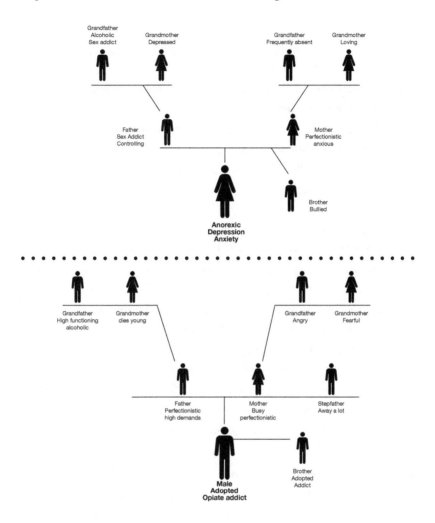

Create a Family Tree

Step One: Name the People

You can start with yourself, the family you grew up in, your grandparents' generation, or even further back in your family history.

While people view genograms with the oldest generation at the top, they often like to start with the family they grew up with. So if you start with the latter, just remember to leave space to then add more family members.

A few guidelines:

- As you note children, start with oldest on left and move to the right with the younger, putting in their ages as of today. Also with relationships, as with Therese, list most current first, and then the others in order of dates.
- When it comes to noting parents and stepparents, also note those who were in a parenting role, even if not legal relationships. For example, if Mom had a live-in boyfriend for ten years while you were growing up, then that is significant. This isn't about those you felt close to as much as it is about those who impacted you.
- Include aunts and uncles if you wish and if you don't know someone's name, such as your mother's brother who died when he was sixteen, just note *deceased uncle* on your mother's side. If other family members have died, note that they are deceased and the approximate age at the time of death.
- This is for your own purpose and only needs to make sense to you, so it's really up to you who you include.
- For now, just note your own family. You can always come back and look at the generational influence of your partners and its relationship to the ongoing family dynamics.

Step Two: Name the Addiction

When complete with names, go back through the individuals and begin to note those whom you know to have had various forms of addiction and mental health issues—e.g., anxiety, depression, rage—be as specific as you can. If anyone actively experienced recovery, note that as well.

Step Three: Name the Trauma

A family tree can portray many issues other than addiction and mental health issues. Again, go back through the individuals and begin to note such issues as illnesses, premature deaths, adoptions, physical and sexual abuse, etc.

Something not done in Therese's family tree, but which is validating to recognize and acknowledge, is to circle any person on your family tree for whom you have a strong and positive regard, and perhaps do some writing as to why you feel this positive attachment.

When your family tree is complete, and this is something that is not necessarily done in one setting, ask yourself:

- What did I learn?
- How do I feel about what I learned?
- What is missing from my knowledge of this family? How did I physically feel as I did this? (Where in my body did I have sensations?)
- How did I emotionally feel?

At this point, you may want to just sit quietly, or take a walk to reflect, or do some journaling, or call a friend or sponsor or trusted family member to discuss your feelings. At some time in the future you may want to further develop your family tree as a more formal genogram facilitated by a therapist. It will help you look at patterns of communication, family connection, and relational ties.

Before you continue reading, I encourage you again to pause, breathe, and engage in an act of self-care.

CHAPTER SEVEN

The Power of Self-Examination

Trauma and its many consequences do not need to be a life sentence. No matter how deep or painful your trauma may be—healing is possible. I know this because I have seen healing happen, over and over, in many hundreds of people during my time as a therapist. The most common questions people ask at the beginning of their healing journeys are "Where and how do I begin?" and "What can I expect?"

The answer to the first question is to begin with where you are and what you are willing and able to do. If you feel you need to take immediate action, this might mean finding a therapist, or a recovery group or program, or going to a treatment center. It might mean simply talking to someone you trust, a spiritual leader, a friend, your neighbor who attends twelve-step meetings, or an addiction counselor. It might mean a process of self-reflection, starting with the issues and concerns you feel the safest sharing. It might mean a combination of these. It might mean something else entirely.

Jordan, who was sexually abused repeatedly by family members as a child, begins by reading about substance addiction in families. Before she begins any personal work, she wants to understand the family dynamics of drug abuse and addiction. She intuitively knows she will eventually need to look at and heal the wounds of her sexual abuse; but she's not ready to talk with anyone about it yet. First she wants to address the trauma that came with growing up with two addicted parents. She knows this will help support the healing of her trauma.

Michael used cocaine addictively and is now a Narcotics Anonymous member with five years of abstinence and recovery. Although he's done a good deal of work addressing his addiction, he is only now beginning to slowly and gently probe his unhealed trauma. He decides to put his toes in the water by going to Co-Dependents Anonymous (CoDA) meetings and reading about codependency.

Other people begin because they are in crisis. Sara has had occasional panic attacks for the past three years, but in recent weeks the attacks have gotten much worse and more frequent. She seeks out a therapist who specializes in working with anxiety, and who also has extensive training in addressing trauma.

Sean seeks help for his depression that ultimately leads him to recognize both a screen and porn addiction.

Joseph never thought of himself as an alcoholic, but when he finds himself walking into a bar instead of picking up his daughter at day care, a voice inside him says, *Joseph, what are you thinking? Get out of here.* He runs out of the bar, and the next day he calls two alcoholism treatment programs, picks one, and sets up an intake appointment.

While it's important to start where you are, it's equally important to understand that if you are in active addiction—i.e., using substances and/or engaging in self-destructive activities or behaviors—you won't get very far in your healing until you have addressed the addiction. Active addiction sabotages any chances to experience long-term healing from trauma.

In this chapter I will focus on the overall process of healing from trauma. Everyone's experience of healing is unique and can involve many different healing approaches. In Chapter Eight, I'll discuss these in greater detail. However, this process always involves moving into and through seven different layers of healing. While each layer naturally leads to the next, none of them has a hard-and-fast boundary. At times you may find yourself in two or three layers at once; occasionally, you may need to briefly circle back to a previous layer in order to continue moving forward.

Let's look closely at each of these layers.

Layer One: Grounding

In order to heal, you first need some inner stability. You also need to learn healthy ways to soothe yourself and feel safe in your own skin. These practices can help you manage your feelings, both when you experience pain in the present and when you examine painful events from your past.

These practices are called **grounding skills**. These are teachable, learnable, tried-and-true tools to help your nervous system regulate and limbic system stay (or become) calm, especially when you're feeling strong emotions such as fear, pain, guilt, or anger. These skills create a solid foundation for your prefrontal cortex to do its work, to be the CEO it was meant to be.

Grounding is a necessary foundation for the six layers of healing that follow it. But grounding is not something you move into, through, and out of. These skills are essential parts of every layer of healing, and you will practice them throughout your entire healing process. In fact, as you will discover, you will continue to use some of the grounding practices in this chapter for the rest of your life.

As you explore your story in the second layer of the healing process, painful feelings will naturally arise. Grounding skills will help you stay calm, focused, and alert so that you can feel these emotions fully, process, tolerate, and if appropriate—when ready—let them go.

Grounding skills aren't rocket science. In fact, you may already practice some of them. Many of them are fun, pleasurable, or rewarding, and most are free or inexpensive.

Grounding skills aren't meant to be used once or twice. Ideally, they are regular practices you integrate into your life. Many people do one or more of these practices every day. You can also use any or all of them when you feel you are losing your focus, your serenity, or your inner stability.

Some common forms of grounding include:
- Martial arts (qi gong, judo, karate, tae kwon do, etc.)
- Tai chi
- Yoga
- Meditation
- Creating art (painting, sculpting, drawing, photography, etc.)

- Crafting (needlepoint, woodworking, origami, bead making, quilting, paper making, etc.)
- Dancing
- Singing or chanting
- Writing (including journaling and creative writing, poetry, etc.)
- Physical exercise
- Gardening
- Spending time in nature
- Acupuncture

Here are four other simple, pleasurable activities whose profound potential for grounding is often overlooked:

- **Playing or working with an animal** (petting a cat, riding a horse, playing fetch with a dog, etc.). Dogs and horses have proven especially valuable in helping people heal trauma.
- **Doing crossword puzzles or Sudoku.** Neuroscientists have begun to recognize how these can improve focus and cognition, strengthen patience, and encourage calmness and relaxation.
- **Coloring.** People become calmer, less anxious, and more mindful when they color. Coloring allows us to focus on the here and now, to employ both logic and creativity, and to use both sides of our brain. In fact, three generations ago, the great psychologist Carl Jung demonstrated the therapeutic benefits of coloring for adults.
- **Knitting.** There is a surprisingly large amount of research on the healing power of knitting, which benefits the brain and body in multiple ways. The repetitive motions reduce our fear and quiet our fight, flee, or freeze response. Knitting also appears to release dopamine and serotonin, two natural antidepressants. (According to a study published in *The British Journal of Occupational Therapy*, 81 percent of 3,500 knitters with depression reported feeling happy after knitting.) Knitting helps us feel calmer and more focused. Through knitting we create something of beauty and/or value. Knitting promotes purpose, creativity, success, and reward—yet it requires no

innate artistic ability. Knitting appears to be especially helpful in the healing of trauma, so helpful that it is routinely suggested for people who suffer from PTSD.

On the pages that follow, I'll provide a variety of other simple, focused, step-by-step grounding practices. Try each one once or twice and see how it feels. Then use whichever practices most resonate with you.

You'll recognize some of these practices as meditations, others as visualizations. All of them can help generate mindfulness and inner peace.

Simple Deep Breathing

Breathe in slowly and deeply, pulling in air through your nose, into your lungs, and expanding down into your belly.

Once your belly feels full of air, slowly breathe out through your mouth.

Repeat for thirty to fifty (or more) slow breaths. If you like, feel free to count your breaths in order to stay focused.

Breathing the Wind

Stand up and place your feet shoulder-width apart, so you are stable. Take a few deep breaths.

Relax your shoulders and drop your hands to your sides. Let your arms and hands dangle.

Take in a long, deep breath through your nose. Then blow it out through your mouth like a big gust of wind.

Repeat for several minutes.

This activity can be especially helpful when you feel overwhelmed by whirling thoughts or strong feelings.

Palms Up, Palms Down

While this activity can be practiced at any time, it can be helpful when you need to let go of a painful memory, thought, image, or feeling.

Sit comfortably, with your back straight but not stiff. (You may find this easier if you sit on the front edge of a chair, rather than against the back.) Close your eyes or lower your gaze.

Bring your attention to your breathing. Take a slow, deep breath. As you do, count to four slowly— one, two, three, four—at the rate of about two numbers per second.

Then exhale, counting slowly to four once again.

Do this four or five more times, until your breathing is slow and relaxed.

As you continue to breathe slowly and evenly, hold your hands out in front of you with your palms facing up. Leave your elbows at your sides or stretch out your arms fully—whatever feels more comfortable.

Imagine your hands holding all the difficult thoughts, feelings, and events that you experienced today. Feel their weight.

Now turn your palms down. Imagine all the troubling energy you have been carrying dropping to the ground.

Turn your empty palms back up. They are now ready to receive positive energy, supportive thoughts, good feelings, and help from others. Hold your palms in this position for ten to twenty seconds.

Slowly open your eyes.

Your Five Senses

Sit comfortably. Close your eyes or lower your gaze.

Relax for a few moments. Take a few slow, deep breaths.

Open your eyes or lift your gaze when you are ready.

Silently, one by one, identify five different things you see around you. Do this calmly and slowly.

Now silently identify four things you hear.

Then identify three things you smell.

Identify two things you taste.

Lastly, name one thing you are touching.

Continue to be aware of your breathing as you go about your day.

Who Am I? Where Am I?

Get comfortable. Take a few slow, deep breaths. Keep your eyes open.

Slowly, one item at a time, remind yourself of:

Your name

Your age

The day of the week

The date

The area, town, or city you are in

Slowly, look around for one minute. Take note of the environment you are in. If you are indoors, notice the size of the room, the color of the walls, the furniture in the room, the height of the ceiling, and any other details that present themselves. If you are outside, notice the ground beneath your feet, the nearby vegetation, the sun or moon or clouds in the sky, the horizon, the sounds and smells around you.

Take a few more deep breaths.

Circle of Light

Sit comfortably in a chair or lie down with a pillow under your head and another under your knees.

Place one hand on your chest and another on your belly.

Take a very slow, very deep breath. Count up to six as you inhale and draw air down toward your belly. Breathe deeply enough for both the hand on your belly and the hand on your chest to move.

Let the breath out naturally and slowly.

Breathe in again very slowly, counting to six, feeling both hands rise. Release the breath and let it flow out.

Continue this deep breathing for several minutes, until you feel safe and relaxed. (If a feeling of safety and relaxation doesn't emerge, don't continue with the next step. Instead, continue breathing slowly and deeply for ten minutes; then get up and get on with your day.)

For those continuing, gently close your eyes.

With your next inhalation, imagine a large circle of healing light forming in front of you. This circle of light can be whatever size, shape, or color your imagination wants it to be.

When this circle of light is fully formed, picture yourself stepping into it and letting it slowly surround you.

With your next inhalation, breathe in as much of that healing light as you wish.

Then, with each exhalation, let go of any tension in your body and any worries, distress, or troubling thoughts in your head.

For a few minutes, continue to breathe in the healing light and breathe out the tensions, worries, and distress.

If you like, you can end the activity here.

Or you can go deeper by imagining the healing light beginning to slowly massage your skin, starting with the top of your head, around the back and front of the face, then slowly making its way down and around your neck.

Continue to follow the light as it moves across the top of your shoulders and onto your shoulder blades. Stay with it as it slowly moves down your torso and into and down your arms. Follow the light as it spreads into your hands and down into your fingers and then out your fingertips, taking with it any tension from your body.

Let the healing light slowly continue to descend— all the way down your torso, then into your hips and buttocks.

Feel the light continue to flow down through your legs, then around your ankles. Stay with the light as it flows into your feet, engulfing them.

As the healing light spreads down into your toes, and then out of them into the air, let the last of the tension in your body flow out with it.

Wiggle or shake your toes and fingers to get rid of any remaining stress.

Healing Colors

Sit comfortably on a cushion or the front of a chair with your back straight but not stiff. Breathe slowly and deeply for a minute or two.

Close your eyes. Take a few more deep breaths.

Imagine a place of beauty and safety. This might be the bank of a river or a sun-drenched beach or the deck of a sailboat in calm water or your favorite chair in your living room or a spot in your backyard or garden.

Now envision yourself in that spot. If you are outdoors, imagine a light breeze in your face; if you are indoors, imagine a gorgeous view out a nearby window.

If you like, you can be alone in this mental place. Or if you prefer, one or more people whom you feel safe with can be there with you.

As you continue to breathe deeply, imagine colors are starting to appear around you. These are colors of love, of nurturing, of safety. Don't try to create any particular colors; let them emerge naturally. They may be blues and purples, oranges and reds, or yellows and greens. Whatever colors help you feel safe and relaxed, let them arise and fill the space around you.

Stay in this place of safety and beauty for as long as you like. Know that you can come back to this place at any time you choose.

Simple Mindfulness Meditation

Sit upright, with your back straight, either on a cushion or the front of a chair. Feel the stability in your posture.

Take a few deep, slow, quiet breaths. Cast your gaze downward at about a 45-degree angle. Relax your eyelids; you're welcome to close your eyes, but if they close only partway, this is fine.

Breathe normally. Simply follow your breath as it goes in and out of your body. Breathe from your diaphragm and belly so that as you breathe in, your belly swells out a bit.

As the breath flows into and down your body, follow that flow with your attention. As it flows back up and out your body, follow that flow as well.

Thoughts and feelings will arise naturally, one after another. Let them arise without hanging onto them.

When you notice you're following a thought or emotion with your attention, let go of it and return to your breathing. This will happen again and again, over and over. Each time, return once more to your breath.

Do this initially for five minutes, gradually building up to twenty minutes or longer. Then simply look up, stand up, and continue with your day.

Meditation and other mindfulness practices can be especially helpful in grounding us. These practices have many other benefits as well. They can:
- Improve your memory
- Calm a racing mind or obsessive thoughts
- Reduce stress
- Increase your resilience
- Improve your ability to appreciate and savor the good things in your life
- Improve your attention, focus, and ability to concentrate
- Increase your physical, mental, and/or emotional energy
- Reduce depression
- Make it easier to break patterns of addiction
- Reduce the pain and anxiety of going without an addictive substance or behavior
- Reduce emotional reactivity and over-the-top responses

- Lower your blood pressure
- Reduce chronic pain
- Make sleep deeper, more refreshing, and easier to fall into
- Inspire creativity and new ideas
- Increase compassion for yourself and others

All of the grounding activities I have provided thus far require no special equipment, ability, or training. However, if you want to investigate something more high tech, check out My Calm Beat (mybrainsolutions. com/mycalmbeat) or Heart Math (heartmath.com), both of which offer useful grounding exercises that use smartphones and other digital technology. There are many apps available to assist you in mindfulness practice.

Layer Two: Exploring the Narrative

At your own pace, with some grounding and stability in your life, your next task is to explore the history of your trauma. As a part of this process, you will ask yourself and begin to answer questions such as, "What happened that hurt me?" and "What didn't I get that I needed?" These sorts of questions will help you undo denial, acknowledge your trauma, and recognize and grieve your losses. These will set the stage for putting the past behind you, placing it in a larger perspective, and moving forward. This will not mean forgetting the past; it will mean no longer allowing the past to dictate how you live your life. It will mean letting go of an old, painful script and discovering new choices and greater freedom.

Undoing denial is not necessarily saying you have been in denial about the fact there was trauma in your past. Many people who have experienced trauma may deny—to themselves, others, or both—the extent or the severity of their trauma. This is particularly true of people who were raised in addictive families. As a child, in order to live with chronic trauma, you may have become quite skilled at minimizing, rationalizing, discounting, pretending things were different, and otherwise denying what was actually happening. At the time, that denial was a necessary survival mechanism, a very real form of resilience.

Now that you are an adult and no longer stuck inside that family system, denial is no longer necessary or helpful. In fact, it will block your healing and recovery. This is why breaking through denial is so essential. As you'll discover, it will also help you be more honest about the here and now.

Exploring the past is an act of empowerment. It relieves you of the burden of holding on to defenses you no longer need, and it helps you discover (or reclaim) your power to recognize and make healthy choices. In addition, being able to talk honestly without fearing rejection or punishment is profoundly freeing.

At first, some people think this layer of healing involves blaming others. It does not. Accepting the truth is not the same as assigning blame. When you acknowledge that you were wounded and how you were wounded, you are helping yourself to heal, not exacting revenge on anyone else. Another common criticism about this layer of healing is that it encourages people to stay stuck in the past. The concern is that when you acknowledge your wounds, you are wallowing in them and reinforcing a "damage model." The truth is precisely the opposite. Admitting and looking honestly at your wounds will help you let go of your past and move beyond it. Instead of staying stuck in your old wounds, you will heal them.

Think of it this way. If you had a broken arm and went to see a physician, would you want him to say, "Get over it! That fracture happened in the past"? Or would you want him to set the bone and protect your arm? Your trauma didn't permanently damage you; it hurt you. Yes, you carry with you some painful symptoms of trauma. But you are much more than just your symptoms. If you break your arm, do you suddenly become nothing more than a broken arm?

When people begin to explore their trauma—especially in therapy— they may find themselves speechless at first. This is because both at times of trauma and at later times when the memories emerge, the language area of the brain may literally shut down. People may be so temporarily overwhelmed with their experience that they become confused and inarticulate. This is entirely normal. Over time, however, with careful and compassionate guidance from a trained trauma therapist, someone with trauma slowly develops an ability to talk about what happened. The therapist helps him or her safely dip one toe in the water and then take it out again, approaching the truth of his or her story gradually. Slowly, step-by-step, in a safe environment, the person is encouraged to access and share details, while staying grounded in the present and in his or her body.

Layer Three: Moving into Your Emotions

There is a good reason why many people avoid facing and healing their trauma: they know the process will hurt, and they don't want to feel that emotional pain. But if you are living with unhealed trauma, you are already hurting, day after day—and you may have been hurting for months, years, or decades.

When people with trauma first come to see me in therapy, they often tell me they're afraid of what will happen when they finally look directly and honestly at their trauma. They fear the emotional pain will be unbearable or they will go crazy and do something foolish or violent. As frightening as that is, the fear is often greater than the reality.

Many people have survived by cutting themselves off from many of their emotions—by making themselves partially numb. They don't just fear a spike in pain; they're afraid a tsunami of all kinds of feelings will drown them. If these are your fears, you must do your work with a therapist, whose job is to create safety, to provide emotional support, and to guide you safely through the healing process. A therapist can both pace you and work with modalities that do not require "catharsis," a strong emoting of feelings so often associated with therapy.

It's important to know your feelings are a normal part of you; they are there to guide you, not hurt you. Emotions are neither right nor wrong; they simply describe your internal experience in the moment. They serve as an internal barometer. Feelings are also highly variable. Some spontaneously come and go, grow and subside; others may stay with you for a long time.

It's important to keep in mind that you are much more than just your feelings. They are an important part of who you are, but they neither rule you nor define you. If you have been cut off from certain emotions for a long time, when you begin to re-experience them they may seem foreign or unsettling or confusing. This is normal. Remind yourself that you have kept those emotions at bay for years. Now you are learning a healthier way to experience them.

Actually experiencing your feelings is a great gift, because each feeling links to an opportunity or a form of healthy power. For example, anger often leads to a gift of energy. Fear links to a gift of alertness. Our feelings also offer us another gift: they tell us what we need. People who have experienced trauma often have difficulty knowing what they need. If you listen to your feelings, they will tell you things like: "I'm sad, I need comfort, and support, and validation"; or "I'm scared and confused, I need more information"; or "I'm angry, I need to set clearer, stronger boundaries with this person." And sometimes your feelings will tell you they simply need to be felt fully, instead of denied or avoided. Many times feelings don't necessitate any decisions other than to listen to them in the moment.

Because the fear of what will happen when you feel is often greater than the reality, let me offer you a brief exercise that can help put this process in perspective.

What Am I Afraid Will Happen?

Sit in a relaxed position. Breathe deeply for a few minutes, until you feel safe and settled. Then gently close your eyes. Think back to a time in your childhood when you felt frightened or vulnerable.

Imagine this younger version of yourself is standing in front of you now. Then mentally ask that young, vulnerable person, "What are you afraid will happen if you let somebody know of your sadness? Your fears? Your shame? Your anger or rage? Your loneliness? Your powerlessness? Your vulnerability? Your secrets?"

What was the first answer that arose in your mind for each question?

Many people who ask a younger version of themselves these questions offer responses such as these:

- "Someone will take advantage of me."
- "People will think I'm stupid or lazy or weak."
- "I'll be hit or slapped across the face."
- "I'll curl up in a ball and die."
- "I'll start to cry and no one will be there for me."
- "I'll go crazy."
- "I'll fly into a rage and won't be able to stop."

All of these responses make perfect sense. You are feeling the vulnerability of a young person who has experienced trauma.

As long as that trauma remains unhealed, you will continue to respond on an emotional level to the vulnerability you felt when life was not safe for you. Your past fears will continue to drive your present-day experiences. Sometimes by just seeing your fears on paper or hearing yourself speak them, you realize they are no longer real. In recognizing your vulnerability, you also have the opportunity to show yourself some compassion while realizing your circumstances today are different and, oftentimes, more positive. Today you may feel the vulnerability of your childhood but experience the strength of your adulthood.

If, in fact, your fears from the past are still valid today, ask yourself what you need for that not to be true? Often it begins by discussing this with a therapist, a sponsor, or another friend in recovery.

As you will discover, the process of exploring the narrative around your trauma isn't linear. Some people start with the details or experiences they remember the most clearly or completely. Others begin with the experiences that are the least painful or that feel the safest. Some do the opposite; they begin with the memories that are most painful or disturbing. All of these variations are valid and helpful. There is no one right way to do this work. Rather, there are many right ways.

Over time, piece-by-piece and step-by-step, a picture of your trauma and the people and events that surround it will become clearer and fuller. Sometimes you may need to return to an incident you dealt with earlier in order to peel back another layer of memory, emotion, or insight.

Keep in mind that exploring your feelings is far more important than accessing particular memories. You do not have to remember everything traumatic that happened. In fact, you probably won't. And some people who have experienced trauma never consciously remember anything about the trauma itself. They may simply sense in their body that something painful and unsettling happened. That is enough.

A Special Note for Men

In our culture, men are often taught to never express their feelings or, sometimes, to never express any feeling except anger. Some men have been taught to not even have any feelings; again, with the possible exception of anger. This is true for many men in our culture, not just those who have experienced trauma and addiction.

Educator and author Dan Griffin has written and spoken eloquently about these and other **Man Rules** our culture so strongly reinforces. Other Man Rules include:

+ It's not okay to ask for help.
+ It's not okay to cry.
+ It's not okay to talk about your fear or loneliness or vulnerability or shame.
+ It's especially not okay to show any weakness or vulnerability.
+ Having, using, and displaying power are central to being a man.

As we've seen, many people with trauma are initially reluctant to explore their narratives because they're afraid of having to experience emotional pain. Several different Man Rules feed into this. These may make you even more reluctant to go through a healing process. If you were raised in an addictive family, those same Man Rules may echo some of the messages your family gave you about not feeling or expressing your emotions.

Many men are suffocating in this box of masculinity as defined by our society. Unwilling to admit their pain and vulnerability even to themselves, men ignore or deny both. (In the United States, if a male is sexually abused, the average time it takes for him to tell someone about it is twenty years.) The pain and vulnerability then fester inside them, creating anxieties and encouraging depression and addiction.

The good news is that many thousands of men are challenging the Man Rules, providing support to one another and encouraging each other in their own healing processes. They understand they are entitled to a safe place where they can feel, express, and work through their grief, shame, fear, guilt, and other pain.

Now is your opportunity to challenge and shake off all those Man Rules that bind you.

Layer Four: Connecting the Past to the Present

As your healing progresses, you will need to ask yourself this important question: "How does my trauma affect me today?"

As you explore this topic, I suggest you also consider these more detailed questions:

- How does my trauma affect who I am as a spouse or romantic partner?

- How does it affect who I am as a parent?
- How does it affect who I am at work?
- How does it affect who I am in my friendships?
- How does it affect how I feel about myself?

Layer Five: Uncovering and Challenging Internalized Beliefs

As a result of your unhealed trauma, you may operate according to a belief system that you developed long ago. Today, these may determine much of what you do, think, and decide, often without your being aware of it. These beliefs may have helped you survive when you were young, but now they no longer serve a useful purpose. In fact, they probably get in the way of how you would like to live your life.

To begin this layer of your healing process, please ask yourself these questions, and write down your answers:

- What beliefs have I internalized as a result of my trauma?
- How did those beliefs hurt or restrict me when I was young?
- How did those beliefs help me when I was young?
- How do they hurt or restrict me now?
- How do those beliefs help me now?
- How do they help, hurt, or restrict other people who play important roles in my life now?
- Which of these beliefs do I want to keep?
- Which ones do I want to get rid of?
- What different beliefs do I want to live by instead?

To help you begin answering these questions, take a look at some of the most common beliefs people who grew up with trauma learned at a young age:

- I can't trust anybody.
- Nobody is ever going to be there to help or support me.
- I am not important or valuable.
- I'd better do things right (or perfectly), because if I don't, something bad will happen.

- My needs are not important. Everyone else's needs are far more important than mine.
- There's no time to play or have fun. I have to get things done.
- It's my role to take care of others.
- I am not capable.
- I am not likeable or lovable.
- I usually screw things up.
- No matter what I do, it doesn't make a difference.
- Whatever I do, it's never good enough.

If you're having trouble answering some of the above questions, try getting more specific and ask yourself these instead:
- What do I believe about my place in the world?
- What do I believe about who I am as spouse or partner?
- What do I believe about who I am as a parent?
- What do I believe about who I am as a friend?
- What do I believe about who I am at work?
- What do I believe about what I am good at or capable of?
- What do I believe about what I am not good at or not capable of?
- What do I believe about how life works?
- What do I believe about how other people relate to me?
- What do I believe about my obligations to others?

As the answers to all these questions emerge, write them down.

In the next part of this process, you'll examine and challenge each of these beliefs. Go down the list you have written and for each one, ask yourself and note in your writing:
- In what way or ways does this belief serve me?
- In what way or ways does this belief harm me?

I also suggest circling all the beliefs that harm you. The beliefs you circled likely interfere with your ability to develop some important skills. For example, if you believe your own needs aren't important, it will be difficult to learn to express those needs to others or ask them for help. If you believe what you do is never good enough, then you're not likely to try something new or attempt to push the limits of your abilities. If you believe your job is to take care of others, you're likely to neglect yourself.

Now comes the transformative part. None of the beliefs on your list is written in stone. You get to choose to keep it, get rid of it, or revise it in a way that is more accurate or realistic or positive. Revising a long-held belief is known as **reframing**. Typically this is done with the help of a therapist, but it's possible to learn to do it without one.

Below are some examples of old, limiting, unchallenged beliefs and the new, revised, and consciously chosen ones that might replace them.

Old, Inaccurate Belief	New, Revised Belief
People aren't trustworthy.	Not everyone can be trusted, but most people can be trusted most of the time.
I have to say yes or people will think I am being selfish or rude.	I can say no and still be a strong, fair-minded, generous person.
There is no time to play.	Taking or making time to play is important.
Making a mistake means I'm a failure.	Making mistakes is normal. It means I'm human.

Now that you are an adult, you are fully responsible for every belief you hold and live by, no matter where it came from. You need to be aware of what you choose to believe today and what you choose to not believe.

You might literally say to yourself, "For years I believed I was clumsy and inattentive, because my dad told me I was. Now I know this wasn't true and isn't true. That belief said a lot about him and nothing about me. I'm not perfect, but I can listen and pay attention well. I'm not clumsy. I can do most things that I set my mind to do. And when I make a mistake, I can learn from it and do better the next time." Or you might tell yourself, "That's what my mother taught me, and it's been very helpful over the years. Now I choose to believe that for myself, not because Mom taught it to me, but because I recognize its value."

As you examine your beliefs, some strong feelings may bubble up. This is both normal and helpful. Pay attention to what those feelings tell you. For example, suppose you realize that for many years you lived with a belief that your own needs weren't important. A big rush of anger may follow this realization. This is a sane and self-respecting response to such a toxic belief. Your anger is informing you that the people who taught that belief to you harmed you. Your anger is also telling you to replace that belief with one that will serve and support you.

Creating new, healthier, more supportive beliefs is an essential part of your healing. Yet it is the part of the healing process people most often skip over and neglect. To some people, it seems artificial or forced; to others, it feels unnecessary. But from my clinical experience, I can tell you this part of the healing process is absolutely critical. So, please, be thorough and careful as you unearth, recognize, and reframe your beliefs. Please be compassionate with yourself as well.

One final thought on this subject: don't assume you need to reframe most or all of your beliefs. It's likely that at least some of the beliefs you brought forward with you into adulthood are positive, healthy, empowering ones. Please hold onto any belief you feel helps or empowers you.

Layer Six: Learning New Skills

Your trauma did not make you helpless or useless. In spite of it, you learned a wide range of important life skills. Maybe you became a highly creative problem solver because you were often presented with situations that were difficult to handle. Maybe you became a skilled and efficient cook because if you didn't prepare meals for yourself and your younger siblings, none of you would have gotten fed. Maybe you learned to listen thoughtfully and carefully because if you didn't do exactly what you were told, you would be punished.

The good news is that you get to keep all of those useful skills. As you heal, you can choose to keep those parts of yourself that you appreciate or feel are valuable; however, there are probably many life skills you did not learn. Some of these may be skills other people are routinely taught and take for granted. For instance, you may have trouble saying no or seeing options or choices available to a problem or being able to relax and kick back for several days in a row. Meanwhile, the people around you have no trouble doing the things you find so challenging.

This isn't because there is something wrong with you or because you're inadequate in some way. You simply did not learn those particular skills when you were growing up. Your parents probably did not model them for you; in fact, they may have modeled (or demanded) different actions entirely.

The problem with not being taught some common life skills is that you may move into adulthood feeling like you are an imposter. In many everyday situations you may feel confusion or performance anxiety. Then you may try to hide that performance anxiety from others, fearing that if your missing skills are discovered, you will be ridiculed, fired, or shamed. You may also spend a great deal of time and energy manipulating your environment—and sometimes the people around you—so that no one discovers (or even suspects) your limitations.

People who have suffered trauma, especially repetitive trauma in childhood, often lack the ability to:

- Ask for assistance
- Solve problems
- Negotiate solutions or terms with others
- Show initiative
- Take action
- Set limits and boundaries
- Say no
- Express their feelings respectfully and honestly
- Listen openly and respectfully

When someone has a history of both trauma and addiction, there is normally a strong emotional component to skill building. Learning new skills may feel dangerous or frightening, especially at first. You may also feel a great deal of internal resistance, often related to unhealthy internalized beliefs.

For example, Will wants to become better at setting limits with others. He often says yes when he actually wants to say no. Will signs up for an assertiveness training workshop that focuses strictly on behavioral change. But Will doesn't yet understand that because of his unhealed trauma and his history of addiction, it won't be enough for him to focus on just changing his behavior. His difficulty in saying no is closely tied to his long-held beliefs that saying no makes him a bad person or that setting a boundary with others could cause something terrible to happen.

Will learned those beliefs from his mother when he was a child. As a single mom who was severely addicted to alcohol and oxycodone, she told Will repeatedly that she depended on him for her very existence. For years she insisted that if he didn't do all the things she asked, she would die, and it would be Will's fault. By the time Will was eleven, he had learned to cook meals and clean the apartment when his mom couldn't get out of bed; to tell people who called on the phone that she wasn't home, when she was actually passed out or too drunk to talk; and to lie to the neighbors about what was actually going on in their household.

No wonder that as an adult Will feels scared to say no to people. It's not that he lacks self-confidence; it's that he was trained to believe saying no could kill someone and make him fully responsible for that person's death.

In the first hour of the assertiveness training workshop, many of Will's early memories and feelings come flooding back. Suddenly he is filled with fear, confusion, and anger. After a few minutes of struggling with these emotions and recollections, he hurries out of the class. He stands outside the building, shaking and breathing hard. A voice in his head asks, *What was that all about? What is wrong with me?*

Nothing is wrong with Will. But he took the class before he had healed much of the trauma behind his fear of saying no to others. He needs to address the emotions he's carried around the meaning of the word *no* to be able to effectively become skilled in using it.

Leslie is often tense and anxious and sometimes has panic attacks that seem to come from out of nowhere. Her partner Vicki urges her to take a relaxation class so she can learn to loosen up. Leslie likes the idea, and signs up for a relaxation workshop at her church. An hour into the workshop, Leslie experiences a sudden, full-blown panic attack. She runs out of the room, drives home, and throws herself into Vicki's arms, where she shakes and weeps for ten minutes.

Leslie was raised in an alcoholic home. She is the oldest of three and quickly became the pseudo-parent to her siblings, garnering control in the home. If she didn't, the fear was too overwhelming to even name. She just knew her job was to keep order and quiet. Leslie has a four-year college degree, a job she enjoys that pays reasonably well, and a committed relationship with Vicki. Yet her panic attacks are beginning to take over her life.

What appears to be a basic relaxation workshop actually triggers her unhealed trauma. As a young child, there had been no time to play or to relax. She had to be hypervigilant to be safe and protect her siblings. She had to take charge and be in control in order to emotionally survive.

A few weeks later, Leslie begins looking for a therapist who specializes in the healing of trauma. She finds someone who practices EMDR and who also teaches mindfulness. With the therapist's help, she begins to finally unearth and address the trauma she has kept buried inside her since her adolescence.

The challenge for people who have experienced trauma—and, even more so, for people with both trauma and addiction in their backgrounds— is to build new skills at the right time. This is why skill building is the focus of your sixth layer of healing, rather than something that you do early on.

Our cerebral cortex (our cognitive mind), often knows exactly what it needs to do to change a behavior pattern and acquire a new skill. But you are more than your cognitive mind. You are also your emotions and your body, and your body is where trauma is stored. Attempts to retrain or expand your cognitive mind are often undermined by the strong unprocessed emotions associated with your trauma.

In my therapy office, new clients often say to me, "Claudia, just tell me what I need to do. I don't want to think about my history. I don't want to feel. I don't need any insight. I just want to move on."

You will move on. You are already moving on. This can seem overwhelming, but it doesn't have to be. You have some control over how fast you move and the size of the steps you take. It's important to know that healing and recovery do not come in leaps and bounds; it occurs a step at a time. You will accomplish your healing one small piece at a time and one layer after another.

So far I've addressed six layers of healing, yet you'll recall I said there are seven. The final layer involves creating a new, more positive, more empowering, and more hopeful narrative of your life. Chapter Eleven will give you hands-on guidance for writing that new narrative. But first, in Chapter Eight, I will discuss some of the specific practices, programs, and people to help guide and support you in your healing.

Spirituality and the Healing of Trauma

Many people who have experienced both trauma and addiction feel conflicted about the role of faith and spirituality in their lives. If you're like many of those people, the effects of your trauma and addiction don't leave you with much time or energy for maintaining a connection with God or a Higher Power. Until recently, your entire life may have been about carefully watching what other people do and then reacting, protecting yourself, and doing whatever was necessary to survive. Perhaps you found your worth in how others defined or saw you or in the things you did for them. Maybe you've spent your life trying to please, accommodate, and take care of others.

However, as your healing proceeds—and especially as you work through the final layers—something may open up inside you that asks for and makes room for a spiritual practice of some kind. I encourage you to follow this internal call because it will deeply support your life and your healing. It will also help you find acceptance, peace, and serenity.

Spiritual practice can take many forms: traditional worship, private prayer, meditation, chanting and singing, attending twelve-step meetings, or simply being in nature. Belief in God or a Higher Power may deepen your practice, but it is not required. Find and practice whatever resonates most with you.

My only caveat is that any spiritual practice—ancient or new, private or public, traditional or unique—needs to enhance your spiritual well-being, not stifle it. Whatever path or paths you choose to follow, what's most important is that you keep growing and moving forward with your healing.

Most of the people I have worked with found that some spiritual path or practice was essential to their recovery. Without it, their healing journey was more difficult, more isolating, and less hopeful. Through their spiritual practices, they learned to trust life as it unfolds, moment by moment.

Expectations in Healing

As you are learning, healing and recovery are processes, not events. You do not sprinkle magic dust on yourself and suddenly get better. Sometimes the process of healing involves taking two steps forward and then one back. At other times, you might take eight steps forward, then two back. It's not a clear-cut, preprogrammed, one-size-fits-all path.

Growth and healing are also like peeling an onion. As you finish with one layer, there is always another layer beneath to look at and learn from. This isn't unique to people with trauma and addiction. It is how life proceeds for everyone who is committed to growth. It is an ongoing aspect of being fully human.

This is not as daunting as it sounds. As you take the initial steps and begin to move through a healing process you will develop a stronger sense of self, and you will feel more secure about yourself and the life you are living. As you become aware of other issues you need to address, you will be able to do so with acceptance and even gratitude.

You already know that no two people's healing processes are the same. Yet it can be tempting to want to assess your progress against that of other people. This is neither necessary nor helpful.

Healing is never a race to a finish line. For one thing, there is no finish line. For another, there is no such thing as a healing fast track. You can't work extra hard and heal extra fast. That's not how human beings are designed. Each of us needs to go at our own pace, and we need to discover that pace rather than decide on it in advance.

It's also tempting to assume that other people who have histories similar to yours are doing much better than you are. They may indeed be doing better by some measures. But this isn't because they healed better or faster or more fully than you. They may have been luckier with business connections, genes, family wealth, etc. You and your boss may have been raised in similar families, e.g., with violent fathers and alcoholic mothers. Yet he is the president of the company you work for, while you are struggling just to show up at work. He has a stable marriage, and you are now in unhappy marriage number three. If you find yourself making comparisons and finding yourself unworthy, please stop. There is a lot of information you simply don't know and can't know. It may be that as a child your boss had grandparents who played a positive role in his life. Maybe he found meaning in something at school that gave him direction and focus. Maybe he inherited the company.

You also don't know what is going on inside him or in any aspects of his life outside of the workplace. He may be tortured by secrets or shame. He may be a practicing addict. His partner may be cheating on him. He may be dying of cancer. He may look at you every morning and think, *God, that person is lucky. He doesn't have to meet payroll or put four kids through college. All he has to do is come to work and do his job well. Each night, he gets to go home and have a life.*

It's essential you not compare your insides to other peoples' outsides or to insides you have crafted as figments of your imagination. Everyone's healing journal traces a similar arc, but the specifics of that arc are unique to each person who makes that journey.

CHAPTER EIGHT

Your Allies in Healing

Healing and recovery are about connections—with yourself and with others. In order to walk back through the pain of trauma, you must be able to trust at least one other person with your healing process. You also need to trust yourself throughout your healing. The support of one or more other caring people can help you develop this self-trust.

No one heals in isolation. You need allies who will guide you, help you stay on track, and redirect you when you lose your way. Your allies will also provide you with a vital safety net, so that when you stumble and fall—as we all do in healing and recovery—you can get back up.

You will need two different groups of allies: first, you need caring people who can provide practical support for your healing. Some examples:

- A friend who babysits your children while you go to a twelve-step meeting
- A partner who agrees to spend $200 a month from the family budget to pay for trauma-centered therapy
- A neighbor who agrees to walk your dog once a day while you attend an outpatient treatment program

These people may not understand the dynamics of trauma or addiction. But they don't need to. It's enough that they care about you and provide practical help; however, you do need to feel safe and comfortable around them.

The second important group of allies you need are caring people with whom you can share the introspective and often painful aspects of your healing. Beginning to tell another human being what you are going through is a big step in breaking out of isolation and moving into healing. People in this second group can provide you not only with a caring presence, but also with empathy and understanding.

Genuine support is much more than simply being in the safe presence of others. You also need to be truly heard and seen. You need to feel you are being held in someone else's mind and heart. The people in this group need to be able to understand your experience with both trauma and addiction. You need to be able to trust and feel safe. Without safety and trust, there is no healing. Typically, this group includes a therapist or counselor, friends (often others in recovery), and possibly a spiritual mentor or someone from your family of choice; however, having just one such person in your life can be enough to support and encourage your healing.

Safe connections with other human beings are also fundamental to a meaningful and satisfying life. These connections can help you feel whole, engaged, and real, regardless of whatever else is happening in your life. In the wake of disaster, for example, the support of others can keep one from becoming overwhelmed by stress and trauma. Above all, if you are to calm down, heal, and grow, you need to feel safe.

You may or may not feel safe around members of your family of origin. It's also important to understand that not everyone who cares about you can offer you safety and support in all situations. Many of your family and friends may lose patience with your healing process or may have a hard time hearing much of what you have to say. This is likely with people who have no training or experience in the healing of trauma or recovery from addiction. Ask them only for practical, everyday help.

When you do not feel safe or supported by members of your original family or even current friends, you can turn to members of your **family of choice**. Your family of choice is the people with whom you have chosen to develop close, trusting relationships. These might include your partner, friends, sponsors, and other mentors.

Together, the caring people in this group form what I call your personal **safety net**. Each of us—whether or not we have trauma or addiction in our life—needs to develop such a safety net. Often, having this safety net can make the difference between living in despair and shame and living with self-respect and dignity.

Assembling a Team of Allies

Seeking the support of others is a sign of strength, not weakness. It means you are able to hear and be heard; it means you can see and be seen; and it makes your life more stable. It is critical for you to find the right allies to support your healing and recovery. It's equally important that you sort out which allies are safe to share your story and feelings with and which ones to simply ask for practical support.

Let me say this again because it is so important: *Having someone care about you, and even love you, does not mean they will be able to guide your healing and recovery.* They could even get in the way. Many times in my career, I've watched with sadness as a client begins doing serious trauma healing work and, in response, her otherwise loving family and friends suddenly back away and grow frightened or defensive. Sometimes this is because they see they need to do similar work, and the prospect terrifies them. Sometimes it's because they misunderstand trauma, addiction, or both. Sometimes it's because they are in denial. Whatever the reason, they suddenly withdraw their support and say things like:

- "You can't be addicted. I know what an addict looks like, and that's not you."
- "I drink more than you, and I know I'm not an addict. The recovery center's just trying to take your money."
- "Haven't you gotten over that yet? For God's sake, it was years ago. Let it go and move on."
- "Listen, it wasn't that bad. Other people have it a whole lot worse. I've forgotten about it; why can't you?"
- "I just can't believe that about your brother. He's always been so kind to me. You must be exaggerating or imagining it."

I repeat: *Do not ask more of someone than he or she is willing or able to provide.* When you see (or sense) that someone can't provide what you need, look elsewhere for it. Also, try not to get everything you need from one or two or even three people. Diversify. That's why I call this group of people a safety net; it's not one or two pairs of caring arms, but a network of many interconnected strands.

Later in this chapter I will present many of the professionals, groups, and programs that can provide you with safety and support. I'll discuss how and where to find them, how to approach them, and how to choose the right ones for your healing.

Your healing will follow its own unique course, based on your personal history, the particular people who support you in your efforts, and the time and money you have available. Nevertheless, as a general rule, recovering from addiction is best supported by group process while healing from trauma is usually done one-on-one with a qualified trauma therapist.

One final thought on this subject: your needs for guidance and support will likely change as you heal and recover. This means that over time you will probably need to ask for different forms of support. This may require changing the makeup of your safety net—adding some people, letting go of others, and changing your relationship with still others.

Your Potential Allies in Recovery

There is a good chance you're already familiar with your options for addressing addiction, which include:

- Inpatient rehab programs, outpatient rehab programs
- Recovery support groups such as Alcoholics Anonymous, Narcotics Anonymous, Women for Sobriety; these meet regularly, and people attend them as they please on a drop-in basis
- Individual psychotherapists

Regular attendance in a support group is all the group assistance some people may need. Others require a formal treatment regimen. For example, this treatment might include a six-week inpatient rehab program, followed by six to twelve months of outpatient support, plus regular attendance at twelve-step (or other mutual support group) meetings.

If your issue with addiction involves alcohol or other drugs, you have a great many rehab and support programs to choose from. There are also some rehab and support programs for specific manifestations of behavioral addiction, such as compulsive gambling, sex addiction, eating disorders, and so on. However, for some of these—screen addiction, for example—only a handful of options exist. (The number of these is likely to grow steadily as screen dependency and compulsive use of other screen media increases.)

There are also a growing number of rehab and support programs for people with more than one active manifestation of addiction or with addiction plus a mental health issue, such as depression, bipolar disorder, borderline personality disorder, or generalized anxiety disorder. These programs are described as treating **co-occurring disorders** or **dual disorders**. Many addiction treatment programs, as well, recognize the common interplay between addiction, mental health disorders, and trauma. But it's crucial that you understand the difference between **trauma-integrated programs**, which provide in-depth trauma work as well as addiction treatment, and what are often called **trauma-informed programs**. Trauma-informed programs provide a variety of the grounding practices I described in Chapter Seven, such as meditation, yoga, qi gong, creative arts, and even equine therapy (working with horses). Staff members in trauma-informed recovery programs are trained in creating emotional safety for their clients and in recognizing and responding to trauma triggers. These are all valuable; however, they do not actually treat trauma; they only help set the stage for its healing. Only a trauma-integrated addiction treatment program addresses the unhealed trauma that underlies addiction.

The most cutting-edge psychiatric, addiction, and trauma treatment program is The Meadows in Arizona, where I have been consulting for nearly twenty years, at its adult treatment facility and as the Clinical Architect of the Claudia Black Young Adult Center. The Meadows offers a variety of therapies that support the healing of trauma, including neurofeedback, Eye Movement Desensitization and Reprocessing (EMDR), and Somatic Experiencing (SE). Its Brain Center is a central hub to the many trauma services where clients will find a variety of scientifically proven, interactive, neurobehavioral interventions that assist clients in calming their nervous systems through brain stem regulation. In addition, five days are dedicated solely to family-of-origin trauma work.

I am a strong proponent of inpatient rehab programs. I've spent almost my entire career working with people in these settings. Inpatient rehab allows people to get outside of their ordinary lives—away from ongoing pressures, difficulties, temptations, and distractions—so they can focus on their recovery. It also brings together multiple professionals who work closely as a team. The opportunity to experience the strength of community is greater in such a setting.

Now let me turn this around. There are also some unique benefits to outpatient programs. The main one is that you can continue to go to work or school, and go home to your family and familiar surroundings at night. That benefit can also be a drawback. When you participate in an outpatient program, the daily pressures of your life don't go away. Each day you may still have to deal with traffic jams, a disapproving boss, an unrewarding job, an angry partner, and so on. All of these challenges make it harder to stay abstinent and focus on your recovery, especially at first. But they also make it much easier to transition out of the program and back to ordinary life.

It's easy to stay abstinent when you're surrounded by caring professionals and friendly peers all day, or when someone else cooks healthy meals for you, or when you don't have to go to work or school and when your addictive substance or behavior isn't available. But eventually you go back to your old life with all its challenges. The challenges are diminished if the family is a part of the recovery process. To help in this transition many people attend an intensive outpatient program for several weeks or more after an inpatient program.

Most people in recovery from addiction find that group-based work—through rehab, support groups, or some combination—is more effective than solely working with a private counselor. However, some people do find they make the most progress when they work one-to-one with a trained and licensed addiction counselor. It's not necessarily an either-or. While most such counselors are licensed to treat alcohol and other drug addiction, there are also training programs and credentialing processes for counselors who work with specific forms of behavioral addiction, such as eating disorders, gambling, shopping, and sex addiction. It is often the private practitioner who helps the addicted person understand that they are in need of specific addiction treatment.

The Value of Group Processes in Addiction Recovery

The combination of trauma and addiction is a profoundly isolating experience, and it often creates great shame and loneliness. Participating in caring group processes helps people to overcome their fears, develop a sense that they belong, learn to value themselves, begin to trust other human beings, and become part of a community. In recovery groups, people feel accepted and affirmed, and they develop pride as they contribute to each other's healing. As people often say in twelve-step groups, "Let us love you until you learn to love yourself."

Twelve-step groups are by far the most common type of mutual support groups for people recovering from addiction, as well as for non-addicts whose lives have been powerfully affected by addiction. In the Appendix, a list of twelve-step fellowships is provided, along with basic contact information. In twelve-step groups, which are free of charge and open to everyone, people learn personal accountability, self-forgiveness and self-respect, forgiveness of others, and how to ask for help. They let go of their shame. They practice mindfulness. Their experiences are validated, and they validate the experiences of others. (**NOTE:** If you wish to be part of a twelve-step fellowship, I strongly recommend you attend an all-women's or all-men's group, especially early in your recovery. Research indicates that in any mixed-gender group, women are more apt to yield the floor to men and more likely to take care of men's feelings or egos than to attend to their own needs. I strongly believe that in addiction recovery, there is nothing more powerful than an all-women's or an all men's group.)

Not everyone feels comfortable in a twelve-step meeting. Fortunately there are additional options, such as Rational Recovery, Women for Sobriety, SMART Recovery, Save Ourselves/Secular Organizations for Sobriety, and LifeRing Secular Recovery.

Many recovery groups now offer the option of online meetings. These are wonderful when the alternative is to travel a very long distance. But there is something particularly supportive about sharing the same physical space with other flesh-and-blood human beings. So when your choice is between a good support group that meets online versus an equally good one that meets several miles away, it's worth making the drive.

I hope it's clear that addiction treatment alone does not heal trauma, and trauma therapy alone does not heal addiction. It's much like going to the doctor with a sinus infection and a broken arm. You'll need to heal in two different ways. While you can begin healing from both at once, the healing processes will not be perfectly parallel.

Do You Need a Therapist?

It is true that anyone—yes, anyone—can benefit from working with a good therapist. All of us can learn a great deal about ourselves through psychotherapy. It's also true that the greater the trauma is, the more helpful and important a trained therapist is likely to be.

But I've met people with addiction and trauma in their backgrounds who have done some of their own healing by paying close attention to their emotions and intuitively finding their way through their pain. I also know a few people who recovered from addiction just by saying to themselves, "I need to stop," going cold turkey, and carefully monitoring their impulses and actions. Others have partly healed their trauma through meditation or other mindfulness practices; from community service; from practicing an art or a craft; from taking workshops on psychology and healing; from forms of healing touch, such as massage; from being part of a theater or improvisational group; and by becoming involved in standup comedy.

Understand, you will not heal from your trauma—or recover from addiction—just by reading this (or any other) book. No book can take the place of live, caring, understanding, and trustworthy human beings.

That said, what will be effective for you depends on both the depth and extent of your trauma and how fully you are prepared to commit to a healing process. I know people with trauma who have chosen not to do therapy and are reasonably content with their lives. While they haven't healed fully, they're doing okay with their work, their kids, and their partners. Many have found healthy ways to manage the trauma symptoms they do experience. Ask them how they're doing and they'll say, "My life's not perfect, but it's pretty good." I would never insist they be in therapy, but would say, "If you'd like your life to be even better, a skilled therapist can often help you make that happen."

So let's look more closely at some of the benefits of psychotherapy. A good therapist:

- Can assess your situation accurately; can quickly discern what you need to heal; lead you through your healing with compassion and understanding; know when to encourage you to press forward and when to stop or take a step back; and help you stay safe and centered throughout the process
- Is proficient in a variety of healing tools, strategies, and approaches (which therapists call modalities)
- Has a good intuitive sense of which modalities to use and when to use them in working with you
- Has worked with other people in situations like yours
- Understands that healing needs to involve your mind and your body, your thinking and your emotions, your prefrontal cortex and your limbic system
- Is able to combine cognitive insight, behavioral change, and methods for settling and regulating your body and your emotions
- Won't solely focus on your vulnerabilities but will encourage you to draw on and develop the strengths you already have—and new ones as well

Like members of every other profession, therapists differ in their skill set. Later in this chapter I'll discuss how to locate and choose a therapist who will be right for you.

Working with a therapist does not necessarily mean sitting down with him or her in his or her office. Many therapists are willing to work long distance using various technologies and/or electronic applications. I always recommend working with a more skilled therapist—someone you trust—who lives 1,000 miles away over a mediocre one whose office is around the corner.

Still, being in the physical presence of another caring human being is better than an electronic connection. If your choice is between making a video call with your therapist and driving for half an hour to meet with him or her in person, then make the drive. One other essential consideration:

your trauma therapist needs to be in close touch with all the other mental health or addiction professionals you are working with. You will need to give written permission for them to share information about you with each other and to discuss you and your healing. Here are some advantages you and your mental health/addiction professional will experience:

- They can easily communicate with one another.
- They can coordinate and support their efforts to help you heal and recover.
- They can share any concerns with each other and ask each other questions.
- They all remain up to date on your progress.
- When you share important information with one professional, all of them have access to it.
- They can better support and assist each other in an emergency or other difficult situation.
- Each professional can become more familiar with the work of the other.

Finding the Right Therapist

It's important to choose a therapist carefully—as carefully as you would choose a new physician, a new job, or a new home. It's worth the time and effort to do research, to consider multiple people, and to find someone who is qualified and who feels right to you. Don't just go with someone because your friend or sister likes him or her or his or her office is conveniently located.

Because of your background, you need to work with a trained and credentialed trauma specialist, preferably someone who also understands and has worked with addiction. Furthermore, because the issues associated with trauma are so complex, I strongly recommend working with a therapist who has a high level of training, either a master's degree or a doctorate. (Don't worry about the particular degree. A good therapist can have an MA, an MS, an MSW, a PhD, a PsyD, or one of several other advanced degrees.)

Begin by asking for recommendations from people you trust. Be sure to explain to them that you want a trauma specialist, not just a good, caring therapist. Also consult *Psychology Today's* useful directory of therapists, counselors, support groups, and treatment centers in the United States and Canada (psychologytoday.com). This directory is organized by state and province. Each therapist has his or her own page, which includes a description of his or her approach, focuses and specialties, contact information, a personal statement, a photo, what forms of insurance he or she accepts (if any), and other useful information.

Another good internet resource is the National Board for Certified Counselors' (NBCC) directory of therapists (nbcc.org). Therapists are listed by state and by practice areas (i.e., their specialties, focuses, and/or types of clients).

Once you have some names, contact two or three different therapists by phone or email. Ask to set up an initial discussion to get acquainted. Most therapists will be happy to spend fifteen to thirty minutes with you on the phone at no charge, so that the two of you can learn more about one another and see if the therapeutic relationship will be a good fit. Other therapists may offer you a brief initial session at no cost.

Here are some good questions to ask in your initial discussion with any therapist:

- How much experience do you have in working with trauma? With the interaction of addiction and trauma?
- What specific training do you have in trauma work?
- What are your specialties?
- What modalities (i.e., forms of therapy) do you use?
- What types of insurance do you accept, if any? (If the therapist does not take insurance and charges more than you can afford, ask him or her to recommend a trauma specialist who does take insurance or charges on a sliding scale.)
- What do you charge? Do you have a set fee, or do you charge on a sliding scale based on income?
- What forms of payment do you take?
- Do you expect to be paid at each appointment, or do you issue bills?

The therapist will likely ask you some questions as well. These might include:

- How did you learn about me?
- Why do you want to do therapy?
- What are your goals and expectations for any work we do together?
- Can you briefly describe your issues with trauma? With addiction?
- How long have these been issues for you?
- Have you worked with a therapist before?

After you've spoken with two or three different therapists, consider your options. While it's important they have the right credentials and experience, it's even more important that you can feel safe, comfortable, and connected with them. You need to feel they care about you, will genuinely listen to you, and can be helpful. You also need to feel you will eventually be able to let down your guard and be vulnerable with them.

I cannot overemphasize the importance of feeling safe with whomever you work with. Keeping this in mind, ask yourself if you will feel safer working with a therapist who is the same race, gender, and/or nationality as you or one who is fluent in your native language.

Here are some warning signs that a therapist probably is not right for you:

- He or she doesn't seem comfortable with you.
- He or she doesn't seem comfortable in his or her own skin.
- He or she is judgmental, agitated, curt, harried, stern, or rigid.
- He or she is condescending and you find yourself feeling small and inadequate.
- He or she treats you as a collection of symptoms or a broken object to be repaired.

Above all, the therapist must feel right to you. Trust what your body and emotions tell you. (And remember, someone who feels right to you won't necessarily feel right to your best friend or your brother.) If none of the first few therapists you talk to seems like a good fit, by all means do further research and contact a few more.

If you have trouble making a decision based on an initial conversation, take heart. This isn't unusual. Make the best choice you can, and then proceed slowly and carefully. Like all important relationships, a therapeutic relationship develops over time. After a few sessions, or perhaps just one, you will know whether or not you are in good hands. Good help feels good; bad help feels confusing, invalidating, irrelevant, or dangerous. Trust what your feelings tell you.

If it turns out you need to move on, tell the therapist you won't be working with him or her further, and then find someone else. Remember, you are hiring the therapist to assist you. If you're not happy or comfortable with the therapist, you don't owe it to him or her to come back again. If you have trouble saying no or telling others what you need, this can be your opportunity to practice speaking up. I have seen many people work with the wrong therapists for years because they couldn't bring themselves to say, "I am done here. My needs aren't being met."

Finding the right therapist is worth the effort. If no therapist feels right, then please read "Reflecting on Your Resistance" later in this chapter. It may be that the issue is with you rather than the people you are considering.

What You Need to Know about Trauma Therapy

When some people hear the word *therapy*, they think of what is now more commonly called **talk therapy**. In talk therapy, a therapist helps his or her client reach important cognitive insights, which then, ideally, result in positive changes in behavior. Together, the therapist and client explore the client's personal story, with the therapist asking the client questions and inviting him or her to explore certain memories, feelings, and beliefs.

For many years Cognitive Behavioral Therapy (CBT) has been considered the gold standard of therapy. Nearly all master's level and above therapists have been trained in CBT. CBT is a short-term, goal-oriented psychotherapy treatment that takes a hands-on practical approach to problem solving. Its goal is to change the underlying patterns of thinking or behavior that contribute to people's difficulties and thus change the way they feel as well. CBT is many therapists' primary therapeutic tool. In the hands of wise therapists, talk therapy can be extremely helpful. However, it's essential to understand that talk therapy alone is not sufficient for healing trauma. To heal your trauma, you will need to engage both the traditional and nontraditional modalities of therapy, as trauma needs to heal in both your body and your brain.

Trauma therapy today is often thought of as a top-down, bottom–up approach. The **top-down** refers to the work that occurs via the prefrontal cortex (PFC). Remember, this is the logical thinking and reasoning part of our brain. CBT and other more traditional forms of talk therapy occur with the working of the PFC. Yet, it is difficult to access the prefrontal cortex when you are in a trauma response as the nervous system is dysregulated and the limbic system is on fire.

Bottom–up therapy is the work you do that regulates the nervous system (brainstem) and calms your limbic system. Grounding techniques such as yoga and meditation combined with more nontraditional therapies regulate both your autonomic nervous system and limbic system where talk has no impact. When your brain stem is regulated you have a larger perspective and develop an internal capacity to feel safe and calm. So a calm brainstem is the doorway to successfully working with the emotional and cognitive parts of the brain. Healing needs to occur from both a sensory and cognitive capacity.

Trauma work always involves a combination of approaches. Most trauma therapists work with multiple modalities, combining them to best suit each individual client. Typically, trauma therapists combine some form of talk therapy with a combination of the following:

- **Grounding practices.** Many of these are listed or described in Chapter Seven.
- **Somatic therapy. Soma** means body; somatic therapies work with the body to release the trauma energy stored inside it. Pioneering models for this type of therapy are the work of Peter Levine's Somatic Experiencing (SE) and Pat Odgen's Sensorimotor Psychotherapy (SP). The premise of this is that when the body emits adrenaline during a moment of fear or trauma, but can't then release it by fighting or escaping, the

person's reaction can stay with him or her for years. Careful attention to tracking bodily sensations, accompanied with grounding and orienting, allows you to release the past that is trapped in traumatic stress and highly charged survival energy. SE and SP are mindfulness approaches to therapy, supporting the body and mind in a holistic perspective.

- **Eye Movement Desensitization and Reprocessing (EMDR)**, based on the work of Francine Shapiro, PhD, is a highly valued form of trauma therapy. The treatment brings together your traumatic memories and positive thoughts and beliefs to help reduce the distress stemming from your trauma. The therapy uses an eight-phase approach that includes having the patient recall distressing images while receiving one of several types of bilateral sensory input, such as side-to-side eye movements or finger tappings guided by a therapist. EMDR is in stark contrast to talk therapy, as it is a process that does not necessitate the client to describe his or her memory in detail. An EMDR session typically takes ninety minutes and it is often a brief focused treatment or part of a longer treatment plan. It is easily integrated with other approaches the therapist might be using such as DBT, CBT, or psychodynamic psychotherapy. The EMDR International Association (emdria.org) sets the standards for all EMDR training and provides access to therapists trained in EMDR by state.

- **Dialectical Behavior Therapy (DBT)**, developed by Marsha Linehan, is a form of cognitive behavioral therapy that is recognized as the gold standard for working with chronically suicidal individuals and people diagnosed to be borderline personalities. There is little doubt that when someone is chronically considering taking his or her life and/or is a borderline personality, that person has experienced trauma. This modality offers a combination of focus and style of therapy as it teaches a series of skills in four modules: mindfulness, interpersonal effectiveness, emotional regulation, and distress tolerance.

- **Neurofeedback.** Most trauma responses involve the repeated firing of neural circuits that promote fear, shame, and rage. Neurofeedback intervenes in these circuits, causing them to fire less often. Through a computer interface that measures brainwave activity, the client observes his or her own habitual mental patterns and, over time, learns to change those patterns, slow his or her breathing, and calm his or her mind. As the person's neural patterns relax, the brain becomes more resilient and less susceptible to automatic stress reactions. A variety of different neurofeedback devices, programs, and apps are available.

- **Energy Psychology.** The name for a broad range of psychological treatments that utilize the human energy system integrating ancient Eastern practices with Western psychology. Energy medicine is based on the fundamental premise that everyone's thoughts, emotions, beliefs, and attitudes are made of energy. These methods do not rely on insight and understanding but on shifting internal state of bodily experience.

  Thought Field Therapy (TFT) and **Emotional Freedom Technique** (EFT) are the two most known techniques within energy psychology, both techniques involve tapping specific meridians (energy points) in the body. Acupoint tapping sends signals directly to the stress centers of the midbrain not mediated by the frontal lobes. TFT was originally adapted from applied kinesiology and the principles inherent in Chinese medicine and the Meridian System, which have been practiced for thousands of years. EFT would then become an adaptation of TFT. These practices have been controversial in the past, but research is now validating what practitioners and their clients have been experiencing.

- **Experiential Therapies** can mean many things, but most often refers to action- and movement-oriented techniques that may include a challenge/rope course, equine therapy, expressive arts, guided imagery, and gestalt therapy. In residential treatment programs, it's often a form of **psychodramatic therapy**. The founder of psychodrama, Joseph Moreno, describes psychodrama as "the scientific exploration of truth through dramatic method." Done in a group setting, one person will act out various scenes from his or her life in a guided drama and role-play of the past, present, or future. This is a holistic technique emphasizing body and action as well as emotion and thought, integrating the conscious and unconscious.

All of these modalities can be researched more on the internet, and certainly there are other helpful modalities such as acupuncture and Internal Family Systems, etc. The list could be exhaustive; my intention is for you to be familiar with the most common techniques a therapist may use.

All in all, trauma therapists are trained to help each client safely dip one toe in the water and then take it out again; this is called **pendulation**, so that you can approach the truth of your narrative gradually. Painful details are not avoided, but shared safely, while the client remains grounded in the moment and within his or her body.

The Role of Medications

When it comes to both trauma and addiction, while medications may be prescribed, they are never cures. If they are offered, their use is to reduce symptoms such as mood swings, intense cravings, extreme anxiety, or exceptionally low energy.

Trauma cannot be healed through medication. Reducing or eliminating side effects is not the same as healing. In order to heal, you will need to work through the trauma and the pain surrounding it. There are no shortcuts or exceptions, pharmaceutical or otherwise.

Reflecting on Your Resistance

Now is a good time to look at any internal resistance you may feel to seeking support from others. If you're like most people with trauma in their lives, you may find it difficult to let your guard down, to trust others, and to allow others to help you. Your fear, painful experience, past betrayal, or shame may get in the way of reaching out.

You may fear asking for help will only bring up painful memories of not getting what you needed or painful internal messages about not deserving to get it. You may have a history of coping with problems and painful feelings by yourself. You may have a past that involved shame and secrets, and in which it was not okay to let others know your problems. Or, perhaps, you may have asked for help, but the request backfired, resulting in ridicule, punishment, or failure. You may have learned that rigid self-reliance is the best way to survive and adapt.

All of these were probably good reasons to not reach out and ask for support in the past. But now, as part of your process of recovery and healing, you see these strategies of resistance and self-protection are no longer necessary and they do you more harm than good.

Do any of these messages sound familiar?

- No one really cares about my problems or me.
- Everybody has their own problems; I don't need to burden them with mine.
- People won't understand what I'm going through and dealing with. They've probably never dealt with someone like me before.
- I should be able to handle this by myself.
- My problems and concerns aren't important.
- I'm afraid I will need too much and others will back off or run away.
- This is too humiliating. I'll simply fall apart.
- People will punish or shame me for asking them for help.
- I don't want people laughing at me and saying, "Wow, you are a piece of work."
- Even worse, I'm afraid professionals will say, "Man, that's a tough story. I have no idea how to help you."
- Mom and Dad always said I was weak, fragile, and self-involved. Asking others for help will only prove how right they were.
- Professionals just want my money. They don't really care about me.
- There are better things to spend money on, especially when my finances are so tight.

- I don't trust anyone. People have proven to me they aren't trustworthy.
- I should just pray for healing.

I often hear clients say these things. Yet when they do take a risk and reach out, they discover—often to their surprise and always to their great relief—there are both caring and safe people who are able to provide support and even direction.

Reaching out and asking for help can strengthen your healing in two ways. First, when you ask for help, you will often get it. Second, the very act of asking for and receiving assistance helps build trust with other human beings. Asking for help isn't a magic bullet. You will need to be discerning about whom you ask and what you ask for. You will also need to allow for some trial and error. Things won't always work out. When they don't, try something different or make a change. This is a normal part of navigating life.

In reaching out for help, you will also discover:

- You are not the only person who has had to face what you have. No matter how shameful and bizarre your experience may seem, other people have been in similar situations.
- You don't need to feel ashamed.
- You will no longer be so alone with your painful thoughts and feelings.
- Other people will understand what you feel and are going through. (Not everyone will, but enough will that you'll feel grateful and relieved.)
- Other people do genuinely care about you and will want to help you.
- Asking for help is okay.

If you are still unconvinced or afraid, ask yourself these questions:

- How will I benefit by not asking others for help or support?
- If I don't reach out, will I probably feel better, worse, or the same? If my answer is "the same," how happy am I with how I feel now?

- If I don't seek support from others, what will be the likely result or cost?
- What are some good reasons to reach out for help?
- What else can I tell myself that will make it easier for me to ask for support and assistance?

You deserve to let go of the pain and shame you carry. You deserve to have a life of serenity and freedom. You can heal from the intergenerational trauma and addiction in your past and grow beyond it. You can feel safe, make good choices, and write a new, more positive narrative for your life.

Chapter Eleven will help you write, and then live, this new and more hopeful narrative.

Before you move into the final chapters, this is another good time to pause, breathe, and engage in an act of self-care

CHAPTER NINE

Family Expectations, Connections, and Disconnections

The term **family of origin** refers to the family you had as a child—parents, siblings, other close relatives such as grandparents, stepparents, foster parents, or anyone else who served as a surrogate parent. This chapter will help you be realistic in your expectations and better understand the connections and disconnections that developed in childhood family relationships and often permeate into adulthood. You may also discover some of the sections or insights in this chapter apply to your current family.

No two families or family members are exactly alike. Put four members of the same family in a room and all four may react completely differently to the same information. Give those same four people a different piece of information, and they may all respond in exactly the same way. That's how families work.

Sharing Your Recovery with Family Members

The most important thing you need to understand about each member of your family of origin is that they may not share the same memories, the same observations, the same insights, or the same conclusions as you. They also may not share your expectations and hopes.

Let me give you an example of one of the most common scenarios I encounter when I work with a family. My client Jacob has asked his parents and his sister Andrea to join him for a few sessions. Jacob begins the session by reflecting back on his adolescence.

Jacob: "Remember when I was sixteen? Mom, you had a drinking problem, and Andrea, you were struggling with anorexia."

Mom: "I never had a drinking problem. What are you talking about?"

Andrea: "I wasn't anorexic. I needed to lose weight to play the lead in a musical."

Jacob: "You weighed eighty-five pounds. You never ate breakfast, and sometimes you skipped dinner. And you didn't start doing community theater until I was seventeen."

Dad: "Apologize to your mother right now for calling her a drunk. I don't know whose mother you're talking about, but it certainly wasn't yours."

Andrea: "I was not raised in an alcoholic family!"

Jacob assumed other members of his family of origin were on the same page in their own healing. He and I both quickly discovered that—metaphorically—they weren't even reading the same book.

As you heal, you will begin to understand aspects of your past that were previously hidden or unclear to you. Once these become clear, they may seem painfully obvious, so obvious that no one could possibly miss them. Yet it's possible others in your family, perhaps everyone else, may not see it or may be in deep denial about it.

This can be disconcerting and painful; yet, there is a good chance you will encounter it with one or more family members. Over and over, my clients tell me, "I'm amazed at how different some of my other family members remember the same event." Conversations like this one take place in my therapy office all the time:

Holly: "Remember on my tenth birthday, when Justin hit Mom?"

Justin: "I didn't hit Mom! Mom hit me!"

Dad: "I was there the whole time, and no one hit anybody. You just yelled at each other."

As you heal from your trauma, you will need to be realistic about each family member in order to have a healthy relationship with him or her. Any particular family member may or may not share your memories and experiences. He or she may or may not be in denial about what happened or about what is happening now. Furthermore, some family members may be intrusive, unreasonable, or unfair. Some may have poor personal boundaries or none at all.

You will need to adjust your expectations to reflect the current reality of your family, and accept whatever limitations they have. Hoping or expecting someone to be wiser, more reflective, or more honest than he or she actually is only gets in the way of your healing. As you begin to heal, you may feel an urge to share your growth and insights with family members, under the assumption that they will applaud what you're doing and encourage your healing. It's possible this is exactly how some family members will respond. But it's also possible that some, or all, will respond with a combination of outrage, disgust, accusations, denial, or blame.

As your healing progresses, you will periodically need to reevaluate and, perhaps, redefine your relationship with each family member. This will likely include resetting some personal boundaries or adjusting your level of trust or intimacy with that person.

With some people, you may need to do this more than once. For example, your brother may be your most enthusiastic advocate for several months, until you mention the time nine years ago when you spied on him and his boyfriend doing meth in the basement, at which point he may make a 180-degree turn.

Try not to ask for or expect something from family members if they seem unwilling or unable to respond to your needs. While you always have the right to tell someone what you want or need from him or her, you set yourself up for disappointment when you ask for something he or she is incapable of doing. When you stop expecting or asking for what you won't get, your relationship with that person becomes healthier.

You will also discover a turning point in your family relationships and in your healing when you realize *your growth does not involve getting other people to change.* Your family members may not change a bit or live their lives any differently or let go of any denial. They may even continue to try to wound you. Fortunately, none of this makes any difference for your own healing. You can heal thoroughly without their approval or assistance.

It is also true that when change occurs in just one member of a family system—in this case, you—it creates the potential for change in others. The changes people see in you may be changes they desire for themselves. You may be a model that offers them hope.

The bottom line is this: your healing and recovery are about you creating change for yourself. If that occurs, you have succeeded and your life will have deeper meaning and be more serene. If someone else heals and grows as well, that is an unexpected gift.

Staying Connected—with Limitations

It's unfortunate, but for many people with trauma, their healing and recovery only further alienates them from some (or even all) members of their family. This is not because they have done something wrong, although some family members may accuse them of this; it's because, in healing their trauma, they are doing something very healthy and very right. Sometimes the act of healing can be confusing, or even threatening, for other family members.

My clients often express loneliness and sadness about this. They tell me, "I expected that my own healing process would help my family to heal or at least would make us closer. It never occurred to me that it would have the opposite effect." I remind them that in many families, once recovery begins, relationships ultimately get better. But this takes time. Sadly, the reality is that there are families in which relationships are never developed or repaired. Certainly their sadness is appropriate and understandable.

For many people, the healthiest thing they can do is accept their interactions with some or all family members have limitations—sharing daily routines, religious practices, and/or family celebrations without intimacy or emotional self-disclosure. If, in your own family, your attempts to create deeper connection have only led to conflict or further wounding, this may be your best solution.

Let's look at a typical example. In Amy's family, she is the only one healing from trauma and is in recovery from addiction. Still, Amy and her codependent mother are able to share weekend holidays now and then. They enjoy sightseeing together, and when visiting each other in their homes they connect through local gossip and conversations about favorite television programs.

For the past several years, Amy has also enjoyed taking walks through the woods with her alcoholic father. She carefully times her visits so he will not be drunk, and she limits the amount of the time they spend together. Under these circumstances, she has found common ground where they can bond by talking about trees and forest animals.

Amy's visits with her two sisters are less frequent; their ways of seeing the world are far too different. Neither of her sisters believes in therapy. They both tell Amy she needs to grow up and forget about her past. One of them has a severe shopping and debt problem; the other is in pursuit of husband number four. Because there is so much potential for conflict, Amy wisely limits her interactions with them to talk about food, movies, music, celebrities, and the weather. Amy would like more intimacy and more authentic sharing with them, but she understands that unless her sisters change—this isn't going to happen.

Amy recognizes these limitations, grieves her losses, and accepts her situation. She has also developed other relationships in her life that provide her with healthier, more intimate bonds. Many of these are with her family of choice, which I wrote about in Chapter Eight.

Unfortunately, for some people, all family-of-origin interactions result in nothing but pain. As a result, they may choose to remove themselves from any relationship with their parents and/or other family members. This can be a healthy and helpful decision for some people, especially those whose families are routinely abusive. However, I encourage people to make such a decision very thoughtfully. If you do create a complete physical separation from your family, be aware that this alone will not magically create healing. It can, however, create some respite and safety within which you can heal.

It is helpful to understand and to be honest with yourself about your motives for wanting to engage with each member of your family. Do you feel a sense of loyalty or duty? Do you experience genuine enjoyment, connection, or love? Are you still seeking validation or approval? If your family is still addicted or otherwise seriously dysfunctional, the people in it may be no more able to provide validation or approval now than when you were younger. In fact, it is more likely they now seek validation and approval from you.

No matter how you define the boundaries of your relationships with other family members, you still need to attend to your own healing. Remember the boundaries of today do not have to be the boundaries of tomorrow. Recovery and relationships are fluid.

Setting Healthy Limits and Boundaries

The challenge in maintaining and navigating family relationships, and your relationships in general, is maintaining the integrity of your healing no matter what happens. This means consistently protecting and taking care of yourself and not expecting anyone else to.

Here are some of the questions you will need to answer for yourself— through experience, trial, and error—for each family member, as well as for family gatherings.

- How much time can you spend with this person before the relationship begins to deteriorate? (If things start to unravel after, say, fifteen minutes, plan to end the visit or conversation after ten.)
- How much time can you spend with this person before you can no longer maintain your own boundaries?
- What conversations and topics will you need to declare off-limits because these only lead to hurtful behaviors?

Please note that declaring a subject off limits is not the same as having a "Don't Talk" rule. The purpose of setting a boundary around a certain topic is to maintain a positive relationship, not promote denial.

If you're still not sure whether to declare something off-limits, simply ask yourself, "Is it possible to discuss this openly and honestly with this person, without rancor or blame?" If the answer is no, then you need to set a boundary around that topic.

With some people it's best to set that boundary clearly and deliberately: "Hey, let's not talk about religion; it only gets in the way for us," or "I already have to listen to way too much political debate over my own dinner table; I'd really enjoy talking about something else when we're together." With others, it may be best to not even raise the subject of setting a boundary. Instead, simply avoid potentially volatile subjects. This may include subtly (or not-so-subtly) changing the subject when you sense conflict or hurtful behavior on the horizon.

Also note that in setting the boundaries described above, you are not making decisions based on a fear of rejection or a need for approval. Instead, you are simply choosing to set parameters that encourage interactions that are positive, healthy, and sometimes even enjoyable.

One other consideration involves emotional support. Before any planned encounter with a family member, it is wise to consider what emotional support you may need, and then to plan for it.

For example, imagine you are planning to drive out of state to visit your parents for three days. Although both of your parents are successful business people who are considered pillars of the community, they are also cocaine addicts. A few days before you leave for the visit, you ask a couple of your good friends (or members of your family of choice) to be available for you to contact them if the situation spirals into craziness. In the hours before you leave, you exercise, meditate, and do a few minutes of yoga.

While you are in your parents' home, each day you deliberately spend one to two hours away from the family house—walking, meditating, enjoying nature, or simply sitting quietly and breathing. If the weather is unpleasant, you find a church or coffee shop in which to sit quietly or a mall to take a walk. If you attend self-help meetings, attending a local self-help group and/or contacting your sponsor would also be grounding.

Connecting with Siblings

Siblings may experience life very differently. This isn't just a matter of perception or temperament. Sometimes life in a family simply changes dramatically over time.

When Annie was young, her family took vacations together, often visited amusement parks on weekends, and laughed at her father's antics at the dinner table. But when Annie was sixteen and Dana was four, their parents divorced, and Mom was granted full-time custody. Vacations and weekend excursions were now too expensive for her mother, who had to work two jobs. Dad, who moved to New Hampshire soon after the separation, was never around. On most weeknights, Annie had to make dinner for herself and Dana while their mother was still at work.

Simply because she was older, Annie's childhood included far more stability and joy than Dana's. Annie still grieves her parents' divorce and has many fond memories of growing up with both parents. Dana, who has only vague memories of her dad, experienced a childhood that was painful and lonely, but she has little grief about the loss of a once-present father.

Or consider Beryl and Barry, twins born to parents who were both successful artists, and their brother Sanjay. Beryl and Barry were eleven when Sanjay was adopted from Pakistan. While Sanjay was still an infant, both parents slowly went from social drinking to problem drinking to full-blown alcoholism. Over a year and a half, the family shifted from generally functional to deeply dysfunctional. Two years after that, the father killed himself.

All three children, of course, experienced multiple traumas. But it should come as no surprise that Sanjay suffered far more—and far greater—trauma than his siblings. Today, two decades later, Sanjay continues to struggle daily with depression. He often tells Beryl and Barry, "You grew up in a completely different universe than I did. I don't just mean that you were born in America. I mean that, for a time, you had a loving family. I had four parents, but I never had a loving family."

When a family's life is chaotic as a result of addiction or when a family is rigid and emotionally isolating, there is often a lack of bonding between siblings, which usually continues into adulthood.

Siblings who grew up in such families are witnesses to each other's pain. As adults, in each other's presence, they mirror the disappointment, fear, anger, and shame of their early years. No wonder their relationships with one another are superficial; it helps them avoid recalling and re-experiencing the pain. It's also often the case that children in such families grew up so emotionally isolated that they have little on which to base a relationship.

If you were raised in such a family, as part of your healing you may want to try to put the pieces of your family history together. You may wish to explore the issue of distance between you and your siblings. You may want to reach out to your siblings now and try to build bonds as adults.

It's important to understand, though, that not all or any of your siblings may be at a similar stage of healing. When you reach out to your brother, he may enthusiastically reach out to you as well, but your sisters may take your overtures as an affront and back away. You can offer your sibling information about your experiences in the family and about your healing process. You can explain how you perceive his or her life has been impacted by the addiction and trauma in your family. You can look for ways to build trust, understanding, and intimacy as adults. But you cannot control whether or not your sibling will listen or care or seek his or her own healing.

In my experience as a therapist, family members rarely heal and recover in sync with one another. Sometimes healing and recovery occur for different family members years, or even decades, apart.

Just as addiction tends to permeate the entire family system, often so does recovery. In healing and recovery, lone wolves are rare. Once one family member walks a path of recovery and healing, usually one or more other members eventually follow in his or her footsteps. I have seen many family members find their way to each other in recovery.

Confronting Family Members as an Adult[1]

If you were raised in an addicted or abusive family, as an adult it's natural to want to confront family members who were responsible for some of the trauma in your childhood. Sharing and confronting are parts of the same continuum. You may want to think of it as a "share-frontation," in which

---

[1] This chapter is about families, so I've written only about confronting family members here. In certain situations, however, there may be value in confronting a non-family member who was behind some of your childhood trauma—for example, a member of the clergy who sexually abused you or a teacher who regularly shamed you in front of the class.

you speak from a place of respect and maintain healthy boundaries. You calmly and straightforwardly tell them what they did that was painful and why it was so painful.

But what's the best way to do this? Is it even wise to do it? How do you decide? And how important is this confrontation to your healing and recovery? There are many benefits to confronting someone about his or her past actions.

- It can resolve—or at least bring closure to—a part of the relationship that bothers you. This closure is important because unresolved relationships will continue to trouble you until you deal with them, preferably with the participation of the person involved.
- It breaks through any denial, lies, or false narratives.
- It provides you and the person you confront with an opportunity to set the record straight, to communicate what you need, and to listen to and perhaps understand one another.
- It enables you to take back your power, to break the cycle of victimization, and to demonstrate to yourself, as well as to the person you confront, that you will not allow anyone to control, dominate, or victimize you.
- It helps you in all your other relationships. Because you have created some closure in this particular troubling relationship, you have put to bed issues that otherwise might suddenly and unexpectedly rear their heads in other contexts. (For example, suppose your mother used to hit you when she was drunk and angry. If you see an adult mistreating a child, you're now much more likely to call 911 and much less likely to step in and punch the adult.)

Speaking your truth out loud is vital, but whether you confront someone in person, face-to-face, is another question. Many people speak their truth in therapy or in a recovery group or to a friend, but choose not to confront family members directly and in person. Others decide to confront family members just as directly, but not in person—via a phone call, a letter, an email, etc. Which is the wisest choice for your situation?

There's no simple, one-size-fits-all solution. Much depends on you, the person you confront, and the history between you both.

Let me briefly review the key advantages and disadvantages of each option. Consider all of these carefully as you decide which is best in each individual case. By the way, it is not cowardly to choose to not confront someone face-to-face. Bravery isn't the issue here. The point is to choose the approach you believe will work best.

The advantages of confronting someone face-to-face are:
- You can see and hear the person's reactions to what you say, in real time. It is hard for the other person to ignore you or the truth you are speaking.
- It offers the two of you an opportunity to discuss the issue then and there, if both of you are willing.

The disadvantages of confronting someone face-to-face are:
- The person you confront may resort to one of the very actions you are calling out and that were so painful in the past. These might include interruption, verbal abuse, physical abuse, condemnation, mockery, prayer for your redemption, calling 911 and reporting you as a threat, challenging you to a fistfight, etc.
- The person's response may confuse, shock, or distract you. (This may or may not be a deliberate strategy.)
- The person may not hear, acknowledge, or accept what you say. He or she may even deny, dismiss, or discount it or discount you. While such a response is possible no matter how you reach out to someone, it is almost always more painful when done in person.
- You may not want or need the other person to respond. You may just want him or her to listen without responding. But you have no control over the other person who may insist on defending him- or herself, insulting you, laughing at you, etc.

> **Important:** If you think there is a chance the
> person might become abusive, do not plan a
> face-to-face confrontation with him or her.

Confronting someone on the phone or other electronic applications has the same advantages and disadvantages, with these twists:

- Each of you can quickly and easily disengage at any time. This enables you to hang up or disconnect if you need to—for instance, if the other person becomes abusive. But it also enables the other person to suddenly hang up or disconnect as well.
- Neither of you can read much (or any) of the other's body language.
- Either of you can easily record the conversation, and neither of you can control what the other does with that recording.

If you choose to confront someone in real time, consider whether or not this would be best done with a therapist or if you are comfortable doing it on your own. Choose a time and place where you can feel safe, comfortable, and alert.

Get clear about what you will say, and plan to say the most important things first. This ensures those things get said no matter what the other person does. Practice what you will say several times. Be realistic about how much you will say. It's probably not feasible—or advisable—to say everything you've always wanted to say in one encounter.

Confronting someone via a letter or email gives the person a chance to mull over your message and respond at his or her convenience. This also makes it much easier for the person to ignore you. (If someone hangs up on you, he or she has clearly and deliberately pushed you away. But if someone doesn't respond to your letter or email, then that person's lack of response is far more ambiguous.) And, of course, you don't have the benefits of being able to see and/or hear one another or talk in real time.

As part of their healing, many people choose to symbolically confront family members rather than confront them in person. This enables them to maintain a safe, protected environment, using therapy techniques such as gestalt, role-playing, psychodrama, empty chair work,[2] and writing but not sending letters or emails.

> *The advantages of confronting someone symbolically are:*
> - You are free to speak your truth in full without fearing or worrying about the other person's reaction.
> - You can ensure your safety and still gain closure for yourself.
> - You don't need to know how to contact the person or wait for him or her to be available.
> - You can confront someone even if that person is dead; if he or she has broken off all contact with you; if you have broken off all contact with the person; or if he or she is otherwise unreachable.

> *The disadvantages of confronting someone symbolically are:*
> - There can be no joint reconciliation.
> - You don't know what the person would have done or how you would have felt—in real life.

If you do choose to confront someone symbolically, you of course continue to have the option to confront him or her directly at a later time.

Symbolically Confronting Someone Who Has Died

When someone important to you dies, there is usually much grief—grief over the pain of the past and grief for what will never be. Feeling and accepting this grief is an important part of healing.

Rita was never close to her father. Over the years, as an adult, she learned to accept his ongoing indifference and his rejection of her. When Rita was forty-two, her father died suddenly. She was shocked and confused by the intensity of her reaction; she felt a great sense of loss, and deep sadness and anger that were physically painful.

---

[2] In empty chair work, you sit in front of an empty chair and imagine the person you wish to speak to is sitting in it. Then, out loud, you have a conversation with that person. You speak for the other person as well as for yourself.

As she investigated these feelings, she became profoundly aware of what she never had and now would never get from her father. She would never hear an apology. She would never hear the words "I love you"—words she longed to hear from him.

As an adult, Rita had courageously worked through her emotions around her father's distance and indifference. Yet there was another layer of grief and awareness that could only appear after her father died. This led to another phase of grief work for her. The finality of the loss pushed Rita to a final depth of grief and acceptance.

Don't Try to Do It All Alone

Whether you choose to confront a family member on your own or with the guidance and support of a therapist, please remember: For your healing journey in general, you need the support of others. Ask for and make good use of support from:

- Good friends and other members of your family of choice
- A therapist or counselor
- A spiritual leader or teacher whom you trust
- A support group

I strongly recommend Al-Anon or ACA (Adult Children of Alcoholic/ Dysfunctional Families) meetings, where you will encounter many people who have had similar experiences. These self-help and mutual-support meetings will help you maintain your integrity and be at peace with the choices you make regarding your family of origin.

CHAPTER TEN
Forgiveness and Healing

While some people are eager to get to a place of forgiveness, others find that concept unimaginable. Because forgiveness has many dimensions, it is often misunderstood or misapplied. Forgiveness is not a goal you work toward or an activity you deliberately practice. Rather, it is much more a gift that may come to you, a natural outcome of your own healing work.

Forgiveness is a manifestation of deep spiritual connection—with a Higher Power, with a group or community, or with your own heart. This connection can't be acquired like an article of clothing; it grows organically over time. Your healing does not depend on forgiving others who have wounded you, nor does it depend on obtaining the forgiveness of those whom you may have harmed.

Many people believe there is a strong "should" attached to forgiveness. They feel they should forgive the people who harmed them. Wrapped into that *should* is this message: *You are good (or right or noble or spiritual or properly healing) if you forgive and bad (or wrong) if you do not.*

None of this is true, of course! Forgiveness is not about *should* or about being good or bad, right or wrong. It is about being true to yourself. Forgiveness is always an act of giving; it cannot be extorted, demanded, claimed, or bartered for. It can only be offered willingly and freely.

These other *shoulds* often get attached to forgiveness:

- You should forgive whether you feel ready to or not.

173

- You should forgive even if you still feel angry.
- You should put others and their priorities before your own.

This chapter will help you sort through your feelings and let forgiveness find its own role in your process of healing and recovery.

What Forgiveness Is Not

By recognizing what forgiveness is not, you will be more able to see what forgiveness is.

- **Forgiveness is not forgetting.** You cannot forget what has happened, nor should you. Your experiences and your pain have a great deal to teach you about not being victimized again and not victimizing others.
- **Forgiveness is not condoning.** If you forgive people who hurt you, you are not saying what they did was acceptable or unimportant or not so bad. It was important; it did hurt; and it has made a difference in your life.
- **Forgiveness is not absolution or clemency.** Forgiving someone does not absolve him or her; it also doesn't erase what the person has done. The person is still responsible for the harm he or she caused.
- **Forgiveness is not a form of self-sacrifice.** In forgiving, you are not swallowing your true feelings. Forgiving does not mean being a martyr. There is a profound difference between repressing a feeling and honoring a feeling.
- **Forgiveness doesn't mean you will never be angry again about what occurred.** What happened to you was painful. It was not right; it was not fair. Because of that you may always feel some anger. You have every reason and right to be angry. Healing and recovery are about getting to a place where your anger no longer interferes with how you live your life or how you take care of yourself.
- **Forgiveness doesn't happen by making a one-time decision.** No matter how much you may want to let go of the past and move on, you cannot wave a magic wand and make the past

disappear. There is a process of grief work you must move through. This process is what allows forgiveness to occur. There are no workarounds or shortcuts.

What Forgiveness Is

- **Forgiveness is to recognize you no longer need your grudges, your resentments, your hatred, or your self-pity.** You recognize these emotions are quite painful and self-defeating. You also realize they can be excuses for getting less out of life than you want or deserve. You do not need them as weapons to hurt others who hurt you or as barriers to keep other people from getting close enough to hurt you again.

- **Forgiveness is to no longer want to punish the people who hurt you.** You have no interest in evening the score. This naturally creates some inner peace.

- **Forgiveness is to no longer build an identity around what happened to you in the past.** You understand there is much, much more to you than your past. It is only one part of who you are right now.

- **Forgiveness is to remember and let go.** Remembering what happened to you and clinging tightly to it can keep you stuck there. But so can trying to ignore or forget past hurts. Healing involves remembering, accepting, and letting go.

For most people, forgiveness occurs gradually over time. Through the work of recovery and healing, anger and hurt are slowly replaced by forgiveness and acceptance. With every tear shed and every cry of anger released, more room opens in one's heart for forgiveness to enter.

When Forgiveness Goes Awry

If you are habitually compliant, go to great lengths to avoid conflict, or chronically seek the approval of others, you may try to falsely or prematurely forgive others who have harmed you. This simply doesn't work. You cannot honestly forgive someone until your heart is ready to. Pretending otherwise only deepens your trauma rather than heals it.

False forgiveness also reinforces denial by promoting an illusion of closeness, yet nothing has substantially changed or been resolved. In an attempt to maintain a relationship and avoid conflict, you let go of your self-respect and integrity and sacrifice safety and healing. You won't get to a place of heartfelt forgiveness without being emotionally honest with yourself. If you say you forgive someone, but have not fully grieved your pain, then you are lying to yourself and to the person you claim to forgive.

Unfortunately, the message "forgive others quickly and fully" is strongly reinforced in our culture and in many religious and social messages. Women, in particular, are conditioned to be understanding, to not get angry, and to lessen tension or conflict quickly, no matter what harm has been done. False and premature forgiveness are not virtues; they are forms of deception.

In her book, *How Can I Forgive You?*, Janis Abrahms Spring eloquently describes cheap (false) forgiveness as "trying to preserve a relationship at any cost including sacrificing your integrity and safety. On the surface you may act as if nothing is wrong, but inside you are bleeding out. Silencing your anguish and indignation only silences your heart and soul."

Self-Forgiveness

When most people think about forgiveness they usually think of forgiveness of others. But an essential first step to your healing and ultimately forgiving others is forgiving yourself. It's vital that you are as compassionate with yourself as you would be with others—and as you would want others to be with you. This means forgiving yourself for anything you've done that has hurt others and anything you've done to hurt yourself.

You may have been unavailable to your children, close friends, or partner, or hurtful to yourself in the throes of addiction or depression. You may have lied and covered up what you have tolerated and endured. You are human and deserve acceptance for who you are in your humanness. Now is the time to show greater compassion for yourself. Recognizing the extent of what you have been up against may help you to pause, be reflective, and invite self-compassion. You may have responded to your trauma in the only way you knew how. You may not have known how to honor yourself or express your feelings in less damaging ways.

If you were traumatized as a child and feel you were somehow to blame, you can now let go of that blame. You were a child. You did not have the power to choose or to escape. You were not bad or evil. Your body may have been violated; your emotions may have been repressed and turned inward; you may have been (and may still be) filled with fear, shame, grief, or rage. You may have ultimately acted in ways that harmed yourself or others—ways that you may now deeply regret. But you did the best you could with the resources you had.

Forgiveness means no longer holding on to your shame. The opposite of *forgive* is *to condemn*. Whatever someone condemns they don't accept. In your acceptance and forgiveness you learn to say, I both accept and forgive myself.

Now is the time to show great compassion for yourself. Offer yourself care, nurturance, and understanding. No matter what your experience has been, your essence remains unspoiled and possesses a powerful force for healing. Perhaps you already sense this. If not, I promise you that you will sense it more and more as you heal.

The Force Behind Forgiveness

As you do the work of healing, forgiveness will naturally begin to manifest in your life. What is necessary for healing is a commitment to your recovery; once you make the all-important commitment to heal, forgiveness will take care of itself. You will find the time to ultimately explore what forgiveness means to you. No matter what your experience has been, your spirit remains unspoiled and free and possesses a powerful force for healing. Ultimately, it is your own powerful spirit that will heal you.

CHAPTER ELEVEN

Creating Your New Narrative

Much of this book has helped you understand the narrative of trauma and addiction in your life. This narrative began in the past and continues through the present. Now you have the opportunity, skills, and tools to write a new, more positive narrative of your recovery and healing. This narrative begins in the recent past, moves into and through the present, and continues into your future.

You will actually write down this narrative, not merely compose it in your head. Find a place to write where you feel safe, comfortable, and relaxed. You can use your journal. Use a pen, pencil, or Sharpie that feels good in your hand and writes with a color and thickness you like.

If you prefer to use a keyboard, that's fine. Pick a font, a size, a color, a page orientation (portrait vs. landscape), and other design elements that appeal to you. As you write your narrative, don't worry about spelling, grammar, or correctness. Don't try to write in a particular way. This is for you, not anyone else; so write from your heart.

There are no length requirements or expectations. Some people write a paragraph or two for each part of the narrative; others write multiple pages. Although you can write all six parts at once, most people write them one at a time, spread out over several days or weeks. It's okay to start writing, stop, and then come back later. It's also okay to later change part or all of what you have written.

Part 1: Describe Your Healing and Recovery Thus Far

Begin by writing down what you have done so far to get started in the healing process, and how it has helped. Start with a specific incident or date. For example, *I went to my first Narcotics Anonymous meeting in March of 2016. That was where I first met people who understood what I was going through.* Or, *Last summer, when I found myself screaming at my husband and kids because he had promised to take us on a picnic but then didn't because a thunderstorm had blown in, I knew something was wrong. That's when I called Lutheran Social Services and asked for a referral to a counselor. That was the day my healing began.*

Let's look at what three very different people wrote to begin their narratives:

James: My journey began by getting clean last January 11 in Narcotics Anonymous. This early recovery taught me that I am not alone and not the bad person I thought I was. It taught me that I can live life clean, and life can turn out better. I didn't think this was possible, but the last ten months have proven that it is. Everything in my life is much more stable now.

Mara: My healing began when I went to a workshop on trauma two years ago. That day I finally learned words that gave me a way to talk about my past experiences. The workshop helped explain so much of my life. Now I don't feel ashamed of myself like I did for so long.

Ally: I didn't really know much about trauma before. I knew a little bit about addiction, but not a lot. Then a book about trauma was recommended to me. As soon as I started reading, I recognized myself and my family. I now have more insight into why I act and feel the way I do, and I understand why my family is the way it is. I also see that I have choices to make about my own recovery and healing.

Part 2: Describe Where You Are Now in Your Healing Journey

Here are some of the things you might include:

- What actions you are currently doing to support your recovery and healing
- How you feel about yourself
- How you feel about your healing and recovery
- How you feel about your life
- How you have changed (for better, for worse, or both)

Here is what James, Mara, and Ally wrote for Part 2:

James: I continue to attend NA meetings. I've also begun going to Adult Children of Alcoholics meetings, and I'm reading two books about growing up with addiction. All of this helps me stay clean. I've also begun getting support from other people in recovery, especially my NA sponsor. These all help me to not be so reactive to other people. When I feel a strong emotion, I now pause before I respond. I also don't feel so guilty as I did for all those years.

Mara: I've continued my healing since that initial workshop by seeing Shelia, a therapist who knows trauma and addiction. I go twice a month. She's given me a lot of homework, mostly having to do with meditation, and I've been doing it every day or two. Mostly these assignments help, though sometimes a lot of fear and anxiety come up. Shelia says that's normal and actually a good thing. I think the biggest way therapy is helping is that I feel hopeful for my future.

Ally: I recently went to a five-day workshop on healing from early childhood trauma. I learned just how much our experiences as young children shape who we are as adults. It really helped me understand how I got to be who I am—and how I don't have to be that way for the rest of my life. Also, I have begun to see an EMDR specialist to help me with my anxiety. For years, I have been so afraid to make any decisions and the EMDR is definitely helping.

Part 3: Describe What You Will Do Next

Write down the things you feel you need to do in the near future. Describe these in terms of what you *will* do, not what you hope or want to do. Whenever possible, include a specific time. For example, *I plan to find and begin working with a trauma therapist before school resumes in the fall.* Or, *This month I'll sign up for a yoga class and begin some regular form of meditation.* Or, *This weekend I am going to download some apps that will help me with grounding.*

Let's look at what James, Mara, and Ally wrote for Part 3:

James: I see myself going to an Adult Children of Alcoholics Roundup, to broaden my twelve-step experience. This weekend I'll locate one and sign up. I want to do some journaling beyond writing my narrative, so I'll begin setting aside time for that. I also want to take some type of yoga class. I also need to clean up some legal things. I can do that with my probation officer when we meet next week.

Mara: I see myself staying in therapy. After my birthday celebration tomorrow, I'm going to stop drinking for a few weeks and see how that feels. If I have trouble stopping, I will get help for that, either through a self-help group or an addiction counselor.

Ally: I am going to go deeper into my therapy work. There are some sex issues I need to look at. I also want to start looking at the sexual abuse that happened to me. And I need to look at what I do in relationships that keeps hurting me. I'll bring these up in my next therapy appointments.

Part 4: Envision How Your Healing and Recovery Will Evolve

This vision might include:

- Changes you plan or hope to make in your healing process later on
- Where you will be emotionally, mentally, spiritually, and/or physically three months from now (or six, or nine, or twelve)
- Which of your relationships will need to change, and in what ways; which ones might need to end; what new ones might begin (or become possible)
- What situations or circumstances in your life you plan to change
- Your long-term goals for healing
- Your long-term goals for other aspects of your life

As you write, please envision your future—and the future of your healing and recovery—in some detail. Feel free to include any plans, goals, hopes, concerns, issues, and questions. (FYI, your response in Part 4 will likely be longer than in the previous three parts.)

James, Mara, and Ally wrote the following reflections for Part 4:

James: I see myself having more one-on-one conversations with my sponsors in both of my twelve-step groups. I see myself getting to a place of acceptance and forgiveness. I will be more forthcoming about my trauma history and not be so preoccupied with what others think of me. I am going to look for a therapist too, as I have some things I need to talk about that I feel I cannot share in a group. I need to work with my wife on our relationship. We both have a lot of bad stuff in our pasts, especially our childhoods. If we find that we can't do that on our own within a twelve-step program, I'll suggest that we see a marriage counselor. I also want to pick up my guitar again and do some jamming.

Mara: I won't be depressed anymore. When the warning signs appear, I will quickly reevaluate my self-care and recovery practices. I will also reach out for help—to my friends, my therapist, or both. If I can't stop my drinking, I will look into recovery groups or an alcoholism treatment program. I see myself writing a letter to my biological dad. There are things I need to say to him, though I don't know if I will mail it or not. I will get feedback from my therapist about that. I will find out the story of Mom and her abandoning us when I was just a toddler. I see myself surrounding myself with more support. I will do more reading about trauma, addiction, and relationships.

Ally: Fear will no longer dominate my life. I won't pick up guilt at every corner. I won't walk around in a fog. I will quit being so hard on myself and practice more self-compassion. I will find a way back to a church I like. I will continue with daily meditation readings. I am working on acceptance. I will stop my acts of self-injury, the cutting and the burning. I am going to wear brighter colored clothes and get rid of all of my black clothes. I will work on finding other people with similar goals and similar backgrounds. I will stop hanging out with people who are critical of me.

Part 5: Embody Your New Narrative in a Few Key Words or Phrases

Please read everything you've written so far in response to the first four parts. Then come up with four to six key words or phrases that best embody your goals for healing and recovery. Some examples:

- Trusting myself
- Forgiving myself
- Letting go of false hopes
- Integrity
- Serenity
- Physical health and energy
- Loving myself
- Loving my life

- Sleeping well night after night
- Service work
- Learning to trust others, but only the trustworthy ones
- Fun
- Creating boundaries

Write these key words and phrases in large, highly visible letters on several sheets of paper. Post these in places that you visit regularly: on your refrigerator or medicine cabinet, in your workplace, in your car, on the cover of your healing journal, or anywhere else you like. Some people have been especially creative, putting their key words and phrases on T-shirts, coffee mugs, the home screens of their computers, etc. As your healing evolves, feel free to change or add to these words and phrases.

Part 6: Envision Your Life Five Years from Now

This part takes more time and reflection than any of the first five, so I encourage you to write it in a place where you feel safe, comfortable, and relaxed. Give yourself plenty of time, including time to ponder a variety of possible scenarios. Most people need forty-five to ninety minutes.

Imagine yourself and your life exactly five years from today. Also imagine that throughout those five years your recovery and healing proceeded steadily. You may have had some struggles and missteps, but you always got back on track fairly quickly.

Now, put yourself in the shoes of that future you. From that perspective, write a letter you will send back in time to the you of today. The purpose of this letter is to inspire and support your healing.

As you think about this letter, ask yourself what you most want yourself to know, to remember, to never forget, to focus on, to watch out for, to reach out for, to avoid, to let go of, to appreciate, to celebrate, to grieve, to finish, to stop, or to continue.

Tell yourself about the ways you have healed and grown—emotionally, mentally, spiritually, and physically. Describe how your life has changed during the past five years. Discuss your new goals, hopes, and plans for the future.

Most important of all, express your love, caring, and concern for the version of you who will receive your letter. Begin your letter with *Dear* plus your name.

Let's take a look at the letters James, Mara, and Ally wrote to themselves:

> Dear James,
>
> Six years ago you were close to death. You were a heroin addict, married to another heroin addict, working in a bar. Today you are in recovery from all forms of substance addiction. And your wife has joined you in recovery.
>
> You have set a positive direction for your future and have steadily, day by day, moved in that direction. You aren't the angry person you once were. You used to get triggered so quickly and easily, and your rage caused good friends to walk out of your life. Today that doesn't happen.
>
> Today you are comfortable in your own skin. You are calmer. You enjoy other people more. You're still not an extrovert, and you're fine with that. But you've stopped isolating yourself, and when you're in a small group of interesting people, you really enjoy them.
>
> The men's group you joined two years ago was pivotal. It helped you realize that you weren't the only one with self-doubts or unresolved anger. You also realized that beneath your anger was a kid who was still hurting all these years later. All of this turned out to be much less scary and painful than you thought it would be.
>
> You read a quotation from Glennon Doyle Melton: "Pain is not a hot potato. Pain is a traveling professor." Five years later, those words still live inside of you. Instead of slamming the

door on pain, you've learned to invite it in and teach you what you need to know.

You've been making good decisions about the limits you need to have with your brother and your father. You realize that they trigger you and that spending time with them only fuels your anger and shame. So you keep the interactions light, brief, and limited to occasional phone calls and a couple of short visits each year. This is working out well for you.

You got ahead of your debt and paid off all the fines your anger got you into. You are now off probation. Now you and Mandy are talking about having a child. You realize that you can be a good dad.

Believe it or not, you are taking some college classes and thinking about becoming a counselor or social worker. I still remember how you threw yourself into self-destruction. For the past five years, you have thrown yourself into health and sanity. It feels very good. I'm very proud of you.

Keep up the good work. You're going to like being me.

Love,
James

Dear Mara,
It's been five years of ups and downs. But the news is mostly good. When things got tough, you didn't isolate yourself or get stuck in depression or give up and fall into despair.

Your anxiety is 98 percent gone. After the EMDR, you found a really good Somatic Experiencing practitioner. The body/mind SE work you did was life-changing. Seeing someone to help you work through your issues has made a world of difference.

You did leave your marriage. That turned out to be a very good decision. It wasn't as hard as you expected. Once you felt it was the right thing to do, you took a deep breath and did it.

You have done a lot of emotional work around your rageful father. You wrote that letter and sent it to him. He never responded, but you realized that writing and sending it were enough. You did not need to see him face-to-face to say the things you needed to say.

And you did find out more about what was happening in your mom's life when she left you with your dad. You went to the town where she grew up and found a few people who knew her. You have found comfort in knowing the truth.

Giving up the alcohol turned out to be very wise. It wasn't easy at first, but you were able to do it and now the serious cravings are long gone.

Life is good. Every indication is that it will continue to get better. I love you with all my heart.
                                    With deepest caring and affection,
                                                                    Mara

Dear Ally,
I really like you. I couldn't say that five years ago, but now I can. Five years ago I hated you. I hated your body. I hated your overwhelming fear.

I hated your shame.

Today I totally understand why you were so scared and so full of shame and why you wanted to attack your own body. I'm sorry I hated you. You deserve nothing but caring and compassion.

Our story of sexual abuse as a child was horrifying and disgusting then, and it still is to me today. But you kept it totally to yourself. I've shared it with three people I trust, including a trauma therapist and my two best friends. I can't tell you how much relief that has brought me, how much that sharing has reduced the pain.

Over the last five years, you have shown nothing but courage and a willingness to change, grow, and heal. After a year of intensive therapy and a five-day in-depth trauma workshop, you confronted Drew and Marty about their abuse. You told Mom, Dad, and Grandpa what they already knew but would never talk about. You did this without expecting any of them to change. You did it just to take back your power and to live honestly. It felt very good, very freeing.

For several months you read as much as you could about trauma, addiction, and sexual abuse. The EMDR turned out to be critically important.

You got tired of driving seventy-five miles each way once a week to go to CoDA meetings, so you started a new weekly CoDA meeting right in town. It's been going strong for over three years now.

You have done a lot of healing and recovery work, particularly looking at the sexual abuse in your past. You still have work to do, but your past isn't anywhere near as much of an influence as it used to be. More often than not, you feel good—

sometimes very good. And, miracle of miracles, you are dating someone who is a kind and decent human being.

These five years have been intense at times. But, especially during this past year, you feel strength and a settledness that you have never felt before.

Thank you for the courage and tenacity you will show in the years to come. If it weren't for you, I wouldn't be where I am today. You are awesome.

Hugs galore,
Ally

The Healing Power of Narrative

The act of writing these responses is enormously inspiring and empowering. It's also only the beginning. For the next three months, please reread all six of your responses at least once a week. If possible, read them out loud. Schedule these rereadings in your calendar so you don't forget or skip them.

After three months, continue to reread your responses once a month.

After a year, repeat the exercise again, writing a new response for all six parts. While some of your responses may remain the same, you will find yourself updating your narrative, which can enhance your ongoing recovery.

Over time, as you revisit what you have written, you will steadily build resilience and hope. You will strengthen your healing and recovery. And you will live more deeply into the new narrative you have created.

Embracing Healing and Recovery

Trauma comes in a thousand sizes and shapes and can impact us in a thousand ways. Yet trauma is never just a cognitive issue; it gets embedded in our bodies, in our biology. As a result, the healing of trauma always involves the body as well as the mind. Addiction has a thousand faces, too. Whatever role addiction has played in your life, you need to take it very seriously.

When addiction and trauma pair up, they trigger and amplify each other. Typically, they create a toxic cycle of misery and shame. People can spend years denying this misery and shame, yet their denial only deepens both. Meanwhile, they pass on the shame and misery to others.

Trauma and addiction were parts of the beginning of your story. Now, however, you have changed the trajectory of that narrative. It has become a story of healing, hope, happiness, and recovery. Your task now is to live into that rewritten story by accepting the truth of your past, feeling the necessary pain of healing, and moving through it into a more connected, more serene, more joyous future.

As you do this vital work, here is what you can expect to experience:

- You will come to understand why you think, feel, and act the way you do. Aspects of your life that used to confuse or elude you will suddenly make sense.
- You will come to understand the patterns that affected your life and the lives of people close to you. With patience and practice, you will begin to break these patterns and build newer, healthier ones.
- You will recognize you deserve a life that is free of shame and misery.
- You will no longer seek perfection or hide behind a façade or live in fear of being seen through and judged inadequate.
- You will no longer feel a need to run from or hide your emotions. You will freely feel and express those emotions in healthy ways.
- You won't compulsively try to avoid conflict or seek approval. Instead, you will make conscious choices based on your own discernment, values, and desires.
- You will learn to recognize and avoid (or end) toxic relationships.
- You will no longer need to remain constantly vigilant and closely defended. You will no longer see yourself as a victim.
- You will set healthy boundaries with other people. You will make wise choices about whom you allow in and whom you keep at a distance.

- You will know when to say yes, when to say no, and when to say, "Let me think about it for a while."
- You will discover the help you need is close at hand and you will learn to ask for it, accept it, and make the most of it.
- You will let go of your painful past.
- You will learn to accept and forgive yourself. You will accept and learn from your mistakes and failures.
- You will feel a sense of belonging to the human community. You will see yourself as a normal human being who was harmed, not a uniquely flawed or undeserving creature who needs to isolate yourself.
- You will have compassion for yourself and others.
- You will recognize the full range of choices available to you in each moment.
- Your life will have direction. You won't feel out of control or frozen in place or like you are spinning helplessly without guidance or purpose.
- You will learn to meet life head-on, without succumbing to despair or crushing fear. You won't feel overwhelmed by difficulties or confused and betrayed when things take a painful and unexpected turn. You will accept that life has its pain and problems and you will trust in your ability to handle them.
- You will live your life from a position of strength, confidence, and clarity.
- You will become a healthier, stronger partner, parent, sibling, grandparent, or friend.
- You will approach each day—and each moment—with greater ease.

These are the promises of healing and recovery. I invite you to join the millions of others who have walked this path of awakening, renewal, and freedom.

I am with you in spirit.

APPENDIX

SELF-HELP FELLOWSHIPS

Family
www.adultchildren.org Adult Children of Alcoholics/Dysfunctional Families 562.595.7831

www.al-anon.org Al-Anon (for friends and family of people with alcoholism) 757.563.1600

www.al-anon.alateen.org Alateen (a fellowship of young Al-Anon members, usually teenagers affected by someone's drinking) 757.563.1600

www.asca12step.org Adult Survivors of Child Abuse Anonymous (recovery program for all survivors of childhood abuse and trauma)

www.chapter9-nyc.org Chapter 9—Couples in Recovery Anonymous (a program of couples working together) 212.946.1874

www.co-anon.org Co-Anon and Co-Ateen (for relatives and friends of cocaine addicts) 520.513.5028

www.coda.org Co-Dependents Anonymous (CoDA) 602.277.7991 or 888.444.2359 (toll-free English) 888.444.2379 (toll-free Spanish)

www.cosa-recovery.org COSA (for co-addicts whose lives have been affected by other people's compulsive sexual behavior) 866.899.2672

www.familiesanonymous.org Families Anonymous (for anyone in recovery from the effects of a loved one's addiction) 847.294.5877

www.gam-anon.org Gam-Anon (for anyone affected by the gambling problem of a family member, loved one, or friend) 718.352.1671

www.naasca.org National Association of Adult Survivors of Child Abuse (child abuse trauma prevention, intervention, and recovery)

www.nar-anon.org Nar-Anon (for relatives and friends of people with drug addiction) 310.534.8188

www.recovering-couples.org Recovering Couples Anonymous 781.794.1456

www.sanon.org S-Anon and S-Ateen (for people who have been affected by other's sexual behavior) 615.833.3152

www.12step.org offers information, tools, and resources for organizing a twelve-step program

Substance Addiction
www.aa.org Alcoholics Anonymous 212.870.3400

www.alladdictsanonymous.org All Addicts Anonymous (for anyone dealing with any addiction) 888.422.2476

http://cdaweb.org Chemically Dependent Anonymous (for anyone seeking freedom from drug or alcohol addiction) 888.232.4673

www.ca.org Cocaine Anonymous 310.559.5833

www.crystalmeth.org Crystal Meth Anonymous 213.488.4455

www.lifering.org LifeRing Secular Recovery (network of individuals seeking to live in recovery) 800.811.4142

www.marijuana-anonymous.org Marijuana Anonymous 800.766.6779

www.na.org Narcotics Anonymous 818.773.9999

www.pillsanonymous.org Pills Anonymous

www.nicotine-anonymous.org 877.879.6422

www.smartrecovery.org SMART Recovery (helps people recover from all types of addiction and addictive behaviors) 866.951.5357

www.sossobriety.org Secular Organizations for Sobriety (helps individuals achieve and maintain sobriety/abstinence from alcohol and drug addiction, food addiction, and more) 323.666.4295

www.womenforsobriety.org Women for Sobriety (helping women overcome alcohol and other addictions) 215.536.8026

Process Addiction
www.cgaa.info Computer Gaming Addicts Anonymous

www.debtorsanonymous.org Debtors Anonymous 718.453.2743

www.gamblersanonymous.org Gamblers Anonymous 888.424.3577

www.netaddictionrecovery.com Internet and Tech Addiction Anonymous 818.773.9999

www.olganon.org Online Gamers Anonymous 612.245.1115

www.sexaa.org Sex Addicts Anonymous 713.869.4902

www.slaafws.org Sex and Love Addicts Anonymous 210.828.7922

www.sa.org Sexaholics Anonymous 615.370.6062

www.sca-recovery.org Sexual Compulsives Anonymous 212.606.3778

www.sexualrecovery.org Sexual Recovery Anonymous 646.450.8565

Food Addiction
http://aba12steps.org Anorexics and Bulimics Anonymous
780.318.6355

www.ceahow.org Compulsive Eaters Anonymous (HOW) 562.342.9344

www.foodaddictsanonymous.org Food Addicts Anonymous 772.878.9657

www.foodaddicts.org Food Addicts in Recovery Anonymous
781.932.6300

www.oa.org Overeaters Anonymous 505.891.2664

Other Fellowships
www.draonline.org Dual Recovery Anonymous (for people with addiction
and mental illness) 913.991.2703

www.emotionsanonymous.org Emotions Anonymous (for people working
toward recovery from emotional difficulties) 651.647.9712

Christian Twelve-Step Fellowships

For a more complete list of Christian twelve-step programs, organizations, groups, and ministries, visit the website of the National Association of Christian Recovery **www.nacr.org**.

www.alcoholicsforchrist.com Alcoholics for Christ (for adults who have grown up in an alcoholic family system or any other dysfunctional system) 248.399.9955

www.alcoholicsvictorious.org Alcoholics Victorious (for people recovering from the effects of alcoholism or drug addiction)

www.overcomersoutreach.org Overcomers Outreach (for individuals, their families, and loved ones who suffer from the consequences of any addictive behavior) 562.698.9000

Please do not assume the word *anonymous* automatically identifies an organization or website as a twelve-step fellowship. Some enthusiast sites and retailers use the word in their names. For example, Gamers Anonymous is a video game store, and screenaddicts.co.uk is a website for film, television, and video game enthusiasts. However, Computer Gaming Addicts Anonymous (cgaa.info), On-Line Gamers Anonymous (olganon.org), Computer Addicts Anonymous (computeraa.wordpress.com), and Internet and Tech Addiction Anonymous (netaddictionrecovery.com) are all legitimate twelve-step fellowships.

PROFESSIONAL ASSISTANCE

www.emdria.org Eye Movement Desensitization and Reprocessing (EMDR)

www.iitap.com International Institute for Trauma and Addiction Professionals (sex addiction and trauma) (IITAP)

www.nbcc.org National Board of Certified Counselors

therapists.psychologytoday.com is a directory of therapists, counselors, support groups, and treatment centers in the United States

findtreatment.samhsa.gov/locator/stateagencies links to state mental health agencies' lists of mental health and/or addiction programs and professionals within each state

naadac.org/sap-directory Nationwide directory of substance abuse professionals in the United States

verywell.com/canadian-treatment-centres-63615 Nationwide directory of Canadian alcohol and drug treatment and rehab centers

THE ADVERSE CHILDHOOD
EXPERIENCE STUDY

The Adverse Childhood Experiences (ACE) Study originated in the mid-1990s and is an ongoing study designed to examine the childhood origins of many of our nation's leading health and social problems. The study represents collaboration between the nation's leading prevention agency, the Centers for Disease Control and Prevention (CDC) and the Kaiser Health Plan's Department of Preventive Medicine in San Diego, CA.

The key concept underlying the study is that stressful or traumatic childhood experiences such as abuse, neglect, witnessing domestic violence, or growing up with alcohol or other substance abuse, mental illness, parental discord, or crime in the home (which is termed "adverse childhood experiences" or ACEs) are a common pathway to social, emotional, and cognitive impairments that lead to increased risk of unhealthy behaviors, risk of violence or re-victimization, disease, disability, and premature mortality. We now know from breakthroughs in neurobiology that ACEs disrupt neurodevelopment and can have lasting effects on brain structure and function—the biologic pathways that likely explain the strength of the findings from the ACE Study.

Childhood abuse, neglect, and exposure to other traumatic stressors are common. Almost two-thirds of the study participants reported at least one ACE, and more than one in five reported three or more ACEs. The short- and long-term outcomes of these childhood exposures include a multitude of health and social problems.

The ACE score is used to assess the total amount of stress during childhood and has demonstrated that as the number of ACEs increase, the risk for the following health problems increases in a strong and graded fashion:

- Alcoholism and alcohol abuse
- Chronic obstructive pulmonary disease (COPD)
- Depression
- Fetal death
- Health-related quality of life
- Illicit drug use
- Ischemic heart disease (IHD)
- Liver disease
- Risk for intimate partner violence
- Multiple sexual partners
- Sexually transmitted diseases (STDs)
- Smoking
- Suicide attempts
- Unintended pregnancies

In addition, as the number of ACEs increases the number of co-occurring or "co-morbid" conditions increases.

http://www.acestudy.org

WHAT'S YOUR ACE SCORE?

There are ten (10) types of childhood trauma measured in the ACE Study. Five (5) are personal (physical abuse, verbal abuse, sexual abuse, physical neglect, and emotional neglect). Five (5) are related to other family members: a parent who's an alcoholic, a mother who's a victim of domestic violence, a family member in jail, a family member diagnosed with a mental illness, and the disappearance of a parent through divorce, death, or abandonment.

Each type of trauma counts as one (1), so a person who's been physically abused, with one alcoholic parent and a mother who was beaten up has an ACE score of three (3).

For each question a Yes answer is 1 point.

1. Did a parent or other adult in the household often or very often: swear at you, insult you, put you down, humiliate you, or act in a way that made you afraid you might be physically hurt?
2. Did a parent or other adult in the household often or very often: push, grab, slap, or throw something at you or ever hit you so hard that you had marks or were injured?
3. Did an adult or person at least five years older than you ever: touch or fondle you or have you touch their body in a sexual way or attempt to actually have oral, anal, or vaginal intercourse with you?
4. Did you often or very often feel that: no one in your family loved you or thought you were important or special, or your

family didn't look out for each other, feel close to each other, or support each other?

5. Did you often or very often feel that: you didn't have enough to eat, had to wear dirty clothes, had no one to protect you, or your parents were too drunk or high to take care of you or take you to the doctor if you needed it?

6. Was a biological parent ever lost to you through divorce, abandonment, or other reason?

7. Was your mother or stepmother often or very often pushed, grabbed, slapped, or had something thrown at her, or kicked, bitten, hit with a fist, or hit with something hard, or repeatedly hit over at least a few minutes or threatened with a gun or knife?

8. Did you live with anyone who was a problem drinker or alcoholic or who used street drugs?

9. Was a household member depressed or mentally ill, or did a household member attempt suicide?

10. Did a household member go to prison?

http://acestoohigh.com/got-your-ace-score

ACE RESILIENCE QUESTIONNAIRE

Write down the most accurate answer under each statement.

1. **I believe that my mother loved me when I was little.**
   definitely true   probably true   not sure   probably not true   definitely not true

2. **I believe that my father loved me when I was little.**
   definitely true   probably true   not sure   probably not true   definitely not true

3. **When I was little, other people helped my mother and father take care of me and they seemed to love me.**
   definitely true   probably true   not sure   probably not true   definitely not true

4. **I've heard that when I was an infant someone in my family enjoyed playing with me, and I enjoyed it.**
   definitely true   probably true   not sure   probably not true   definitely not true

5. **When I was a child, there were relatives in my family who made me feel better if I was sad or worried.**
   definitely true   probably true   not sure   probably not true   definitely not true

6. **When I was a child, neighbors or my friends' parents seemed to like me.**
   definitely true   probably true   not sure   probably not true   definitely not true

7. **When I was a child, teachers, coaches, youth leaders, or ministers were there to help me.**
   definitely true   probably true   not sure   probably not true   definitely not true

8. **Someone in my family cared about how I was doing in school.**
    definitely true   probably true   not sure   probably not true   definitely not true

9. **My family, neighbors, and friends talked often about making our lives better.**
    definitely true   probably true   not sure   probably not true   definitely not true

10. **We had rules in our house and were expected to keep them.**
    definitely true   probably true   not sure   probably not true   definitely not true

11. **When I felt really bad, I could almost always find someone I trusted to talk to.**
    definitely true   probably true   not sure   probably not true   definitely not true

12. **As a youth, people noticed that I was capable and could get things done.**
    definitely true   probably true   not sure   probably not true   definitely not true

13. **I was independent and a go-getter.**
    definitely true   probably true   not sure   probably not true   definitely not true

14. **I believe that life is what you make it.**
    definitely true   probably true   not sure   probably not true   definitely not true

- How many of these protective factors did I have as a child and youth?

- How many were definitely true or probably true?

- Of those I listed, how many are still true for me?

http://acestoohigh.com/got-your-ace-score/